THE TRUTH ABOUT
THE EARLY CHURCH

By the same author

Thessalonians (*The Moffatt Commentary*)
The Rediscovery of the Bible
One Volume Bible Commentary
The Life and Teaching of Jesus (*series Knowing Christianity*)
The Truth about Jesus
Apostle Extraordinary: The Life and Letters of St. Paul
The Christian Faith in Art (*with Eric Newton*)
The Plain Man Looks at the Bible
Thessalonians (*Torch Commentaries*)
Hebrews (*Torch Commentaries*)
Jeremiah and Ezekiel (*Bible Guides*)
Galatians (*Cambridge Commentary*)
The Bible Companion (*ed.*)

Translated by William Neil

The Bible as History—Keller
Jesus Lived Here—Bruir and Giegel

THE TRUTH ABOUT THE EARLY CHURCH

by

WILLIAM NEIL

HODDER AND STOUGHTON

COPYRIGHT © 1970 BY WILLIAM NEIL

FIRST PRINTED 1970

ISBN 0 340 12852 6

*Printed in Great Britain
for Hodder and Stoughton Limited,
St. Paul's House, Warwick Lane, London E.C.4,
by Richard Clay (The Chaucer Press), Ltd.,
Bungay, Suffolk*

PREFACE

THE contents of this book formed a series of six public lectures delivered at New College in the University of Edinburgh in October 1967 under the title of 'The Apostolic Age'. I am grateful to the Trustees of the Croall Lectureship for the honour they have done me in inviting me to give these lectures and to the Faculty of Divinity at Edinburgh University for their kindness and hospitality on that occasion.

WILLIAM NEIL

University of Nottingham
September 1969

CONTENTS

I. THE BOOK OF *ACTS* TODAY

THERE are several very good reasons why the book of *Acts* should be the subject of a series of public lectures at the present time. It is difficult to estimate how much the man in the pew is affected by current theological controversy. But even if we concede that there is a hard core of common sense in the ordinary layman which prevents his faith from being shattered by the latest trumpetings of theological rogue elephants, it is unlikely that he is altogether unaffected.

The man in the pew—or more properly nowadays the man behind the newspaper or in front of the telly—is less able than the minister in his study to weigh up the pros and cons of the arguments advanced by Bultmann and his followers, Tillich and his disciples and the 'Death of God' brigade. What does filter through is a general sense that the Bible is discredited, the creeds are old hat and that the most we can say about Jesus is that He was the incarnation of the Good Samaritan. If John Allegro, an acknowledged authority on the Dead Sea Scrolls, proclaims in the daily press that the Scrolls prove the gospels to be nothing more than the extravagances of 'Christian myth-makers', how can the ordinary citizen resist the impression that he may be right? And if in so many of its religious discussion programmes the B.B.C. considers it to be its duty to pose questions to which no answers are given, can we be surprised if the genuine enquirer is left bewildered and unsatisfied? When our bugle gives such an indistinct sound we cannot wonder that so many students of all faculties take refuge in fundamentalism, and, in Walter Lippmann's memorable phrase, welcome manacles to prevent their hands from shaking; or that the less intelligent seek such spurious certainties as bodies like the Jehovah's Witnesses claim to provide.

At such a time of theological confusion there is much to be said for taking a look at the rock from which we were hewn and the quarry from which we were dug. The book of *Acts* covers the first thirty momentous years of the Church's story. What does it tell us of the beliefs of the earliest Christians? How did *they* see man's place in the universe, and the role of the Church in the world? What did they mean when they used the word 'God', and what significance did they attach to the person and work of Christ? We may indeed find that the precise way in which they expressed their beliefs was conditioned by factors which are no longer operative or relevant in our own day, but at least we ought to examine the basic convictions of that handful of men and women who laid the foundations of Christendom.

From another angle the book of *Acts* may have something pertinent to say to us today. Since Pope John gave a new impetus to ecumenical thinking and enlarged the possible field of co-operation between the various branches of the Church in a way that would have seemed unbelievable even ten short years ago, questions as to the form of the Church have taken on a new urgency. Presumably no Roman Catholic would claim that the Papacy in its present form was an essential feature of the Church in New Testament times, nor would Presbyterians justify Kirk Sessions on similar grounds, though they might be tempted to make even more extravagant claims based on the inclusion by the author of *Hebrews* of the General Assembly among the inmates of the heavenly Jerusalem.

But can we find in the record of this first stage in Christian history any clear indication of how the Church was organised, of the importance attached to an authorised ministry, and the administration of the sacraments? How far were these matters regarded as being of the essence of the Church? Do we find evidence of apostolic succession, the three-fold ministry, parity of ministry or any other structure of Church government which might be claimed to be of the very substance of the Church's life and therefore incumbent on all Christians to accept as a precondition of unity?

Or again, it is beyond dispute that all branches of the Church are at the moment experiencing the full blast of the winds of change. Despite a vast amount of unspectacular work for the cause of Christ by clergy and laity in all denominations, congregations dwindle, young people drift away mostly to nothing in particular, religious education in schools is radically questioned, students who are challenged by society's plight increasingly choose other avenues of service than the ordained ministry of the Church. The older generation looks back on the pre-1914 era as an ecclesiastical para-

dise that has gone beyond recall and sighs for a past
heyday of family worship, crowded pews, powerful
preaching and missionary enthusiasm.

Was that the true face of the Church? Were the
Victorians moved by the Spirit like the early Christians
in ways which we ought to try to recapture and
emulate? Or must we not rather in this sphere too look
back to the fountainhead of our faith and try to learn
from the record of the earliest days of the Church's
witness to Christ where our real emphasis must lie and
in what the real life of the Church consists? Nostalgia is
by definition unhealthy, yet it is difficult to suppress it
when we picture in our mind's eye the buoyancy and
exhilaration which are reputed to have characterised
the early Church, and the sense of purpose which swept
it forward to turn the world upside down. But is this
picture the true one? Were there no thorns in that
garden of roses which we may note for our comfort?

Then there is the perennial problem of St. Paul. To
some he is the evil genius who perverted the simple
message of Jesus and turned Christianity into a baffling
complex of dogmas which has little meaning in the
modern world. To others he is the supreme interpreter
of the human situation in this or any other century, and
the man who has understood better than anyone since
his day the role of Jesus Christ in the divine economy.
The book of *Acts* has much to say about St. Paul, as
also about the other members of the apostolic band, the
Twelve and their associates. What sort of men were
they? Can we get any clear impression of these founding fathers of the Church as lively, colourful characters

before they became immobilised in statuary and stained glass windows?

These then are some of the topics with which we shall be concerned in this course of lectures. But of course a prior concern must be the book of *Acts* itself and its author. What sort of book is it and why was it written at all? What sort of person was the writer and where did he get his information? Are we dealing with a historian in the modern sense who has taken it upon himself to write an account of the first thirty years of the Church's existence, who has sifted his evidence, verified his sources, read all that there is to be read on the subject and then sat down to write his book?

Or, on the other hand, as has been more recently suggested, was the author of the book of *Acts* far more of a theologian than a historian, with a fixed theological pattern in his mind into which he fitted such information as had come his way, but with no real concern to set down as objectively as he could the course of events between, say, A.D. 30 and 60? This is indeed a crucial question, for upon our answer to it turns the whole issue of the reliability of the story which the book of *Acts* has to tell.

There was a time, of course, when this question would never have been raised. The literal infallibility of the scriptures was a sufficient formula to stifle all intelligent enquiry. Now that this panacea has been found wanting, what are we left with? I believe myself that we are left with something far better, something which affirms what is the essential character of the whole Bible, namely that it is the Word of God conveyed to man by human hands. Luther said the Bible was written for men with a head upon their shoulders, and William Robertson Smith added: 'We need never tremble *for* the Word of God, though we may tremble *at* it and the demands which it makes upon our faith and courage.'

If I may be allowed two further quotations, which seem to me to bring us nearer to the heart of the matter, I would draw your attention to a sentence or two in J. D. Smart's *The Interpretation of Scripture*:[1] 'It is just because the prophets and apostles are so indwelt by the Spirit of God that they are so robustly, freely, independently and concretely human. The incoming of God's Spirit does not eliminate their human qualities so that they become mere puppets of God, but in the fullest sense it makes them *men* of God.' This, he suggests, is the real meaning of verbal inspiration, which is a far different thing from literal infallibility. My second quotation is from J. K. S. Reid's *The Authority of Scripture*: 'The authority of the Bible reposes in the fact that, in statements some right and some wrong, and in practical application some of which is disputable and some even more dubious, a unified witness is borne to Him who is at the centre of the Gospel.'[2]

But can we ask no more of any New Testament writer than that he should be a man indwelt by the Spirit of God and that he should bear honest witness to Christ based on his own knowledge and experience? The fact that our author was a man of God in this sense needs no substantiation apart from the book that he has written,

[1] (London, 1961), p. 196. [2] (London, 1957), p. 267.

and in his preface he certainly makes no claim to be infallible. Rather he describes himself modestly as one who to the best of his ability has sifted the evidence that is available to him and out of these materials has compiled his book. But the writer of the book of *Acts* might well be a man in whom the Spirit of God was mightily at work, and he might also have marshalled his evidence with care as he claims before setting out to write his book, but if the information at his disposal was of doubtful value or if he had some particular theological axe to grind which made him alter the facts of the case to fit his theory, can we be satisfied that the end product is in any sense a reliable account of the beginnings of Christianity?

Like most other questions of New Testament criticism this was first raised by the Tübingen school towards the middle of last century. Until then the traditional view since the days of the Christian Fathers had been that the book of *Acts* was the second part of a two-volume work by Luke, the beloved physician referred to in Paul's letters,[3] the companion of his missionary journeys. After writing the third gospel, it was held, Luke proceeded to write a sequel dealing with the birth of the Church and the story of its progress from the first Whitsunday, until about thirty years later when the work of Christian missionaries, notably St. Paul, had brought the new faith from Asia through Europe and into the nerve centre of the Empire, Rome itself. Since Luke had been deeply involved in all this there was never any suggestion that the book of *Acts* was any-

[3] *Col.* 4:14; 2 *Tim.* 4:11.

thing but a factual narrative, compiled soon after the events it describes by a man who was a first-hand authority for those incidents in the story in which he himself had played some part, and who for the rest of it was in an excellent position to get accurate information from his many missionary contacts.

The Tübingen school, however, would have none of this. They were convinced that in the early Church the conflict between the Jewish Christians, led by Peter, and the Gentile Christians, led by Paul, was acute and bitter. But this is not the situation which is described in the book of *Acts*, where there is certainly tension between the two parties but also a willingness on both sides to compromise for the good of the Church. *Acts* must therefore be wrong. It could not have been written by a companion of Paul since he would of course have known that the Tübingen scholars were right in their assessment of the true situation. It must therefore have been written about a century after the events it describes, when the early ecclesiastical storms had subsided. *Acts* is thus a conciliatory document designed to bring the two parties into harmony by making Paul behave like Peter, and Peter behave like Paul. It has therefore no historical value worth speaking of.

Scholars on the continent and in this country, notably J. B. Lightfoot, were not slow to point out that the Tübingen school were guilty of the very crime of which they accused the author of *Acts*, namely that of distorting evidence in subservience to some preconceived idea. Then towards the end of the last century came the dramatic conclusions of Sir William Ramsay, conclusions which were based on his own archaeological investigations in Asia Minor. He had begun by assuming that *Acts* was an untrustworthy second-century production, but was forced on the evidence of his own explorations to take the view that not only was *Acts* written by Luke, the companion of Paul, but also that his accurate knowledge of local customs and official terminology proved him to be a thoroughly reliable historian of the life of the early Church.

This rehabilitation of *Acts* was furthered in the first half of this century by two great New Testament scholars, Adolf Harnack and B. H. Streeter. Both of them maintained, like Ramsay, that the traditional view of the author was correct, that the book was written in the first century and not the second, and that by and large it is an authentic and factual record of what actually happened. Dissenting voices were certainly heard in this period. Johannes Weiss in Germany and A. C. Clark in this country both argued that Luke was not the author, and in their great five-volume work on *The Beginnings of Christianity* Foakes Jackson and Kirsopp Lake took a generally sceptical view of the value of *Acts* as history. Most English-speaking scholars, however, felt that despite the enormous value of some sections of this vast production, and the mass of learning which it gathers together, the editors themselves did no service to the status of the work as a standard classic by their innate radical approach to almost every question at issue.

Accordingly, when A. M. Hunter came to assess the

state of scholarly opinion on the book of *Acts* in 1950 he could rightly claim that the ghosts of Tübingen had been well and truly laid. One of our best New Testament scholars, W. L. Knox, had written, just two years before, a small but erudite volume on *The Acts of the Apostles* in which he had cogently argued the case for the traditional view of the author, admitting some carelessness in presentation, but defending the essential reliability of his narrative. Within a century the discussion seemed to have come full circle. Luke the historian was in 1950 firmly re-established.

But as Stephen Neill says: 'One of the curious features in German theology is that no ghost is ever laid',[4] and we have had ample evidence of this in the field of Lucan studies in the past fifteen years. C. K. Barrett in his excellent little book on *Luke the Historian in Recent Study*, published in 1961, says this: 'A generation ago, in his inaugural lecture at Cambridge' (that was in 1936) 'Profesoor Dodd could claim that the Fourth Gospel constituted the most acute and pressing problem in New Testament studies. If this is less true today, the change is due to a great extent to Professor Dodd's own labour and scholarship. It would not be far wrong to say that the focus of New Testament studies is now moving to the Lucan writings. The Fourth Gospel raised, in one form, the problem which is always pressed upon the Christian thinker by the nature of his subject, namely, that of the relation between history and theology. It is the same ultimate problem that the

[4] *The Interpretation of the New Testament 1861–1961* (Oxford, 1964), p. 58.

Lucan writings raise, though they raise it in a different way.'[5]

Barrett went on to say that 'recent years have witnessed a revolution in Lucan studies', and when we ask what has emerged from the revolution we find that 'Luke the historian' has given place to 'Luke the theologian'. Sir William Ramsay's picture of Luke as the meticulous cicerone who guides us along the shipping routes of the ancient world, who is at home in the intricacies of Roman provincial administration, who has a passion for geographical detail and may be relied on to have checked up on the dates of the emperors, has been replaced by the picture of the author of *Acts* as a missionary preacher, a creative theologian, a writer whose main concern is not with historical accuracy but with the proclamation of the gospel, and who is quite prepared to sacrifice the factual accuracy of his narrative to didactic considerations.

C. F. Evans first drew the attention of English-speaking readers to this characteristic in 1955 in an essay on 'The Central Section of St. Luke's Gospel'. In it he sought to show that in the heart of the third gospel where the evangelist is dealing with Jesus' final journey to Jerusalem and where even the casual reader is struck by the recurring refrain: 'He steadfastly set his face to go to Jerusalem', 'as they were on the way to Jerusalem', 'He went on before going up to Jerusalem', it was not just a factual record of events that Luke was concerned with but something much more subtle. Being convinced like all Christian evangelists that Jesus was 'the prophet

[5] (London), p. 50.

like unto Moses', Luke, says Evans, 'has selected and ordered his material with a view to presenting it as a Christian Deuteronomy'.[6] Jesus, like Moses, has embarked on a journey to the Promised Land, and in parallel columns Evans sets the events and topics of Deuteronomy side by side with those in Luke's account of Jesus' last journey. He who is greater than Moses is on His way to accomplish a greater deliverance (Luke uses the very word 'exodus' in connection with Jesus' death) beyond which lies His Ascension, corresponding to the traditional Assumption of Moses.

We may question minor points in Evans' argument, but he seems to make a case for revising our traditional estimate of Luke as the 'careful historian'. This new look at Luke had been anticipated on a larger scale in Germany two years earlier in Hans Conzelmann's important study of *Luke–Acts* which he called *Die Mitte der Zeit*, 'The Centre of Time', and which did not appear in an English translation until 1960 under the more pedestrian title of *The Theology of St. Luke*.

Conzelmann maintains that the author of this two-volume work *Luke–Acts* was writing at a time when the expectation of an immediate Second Advent of Christ had died down. Mark ended his gospel on a note of expectancy, the Parousia was not far off, the end of the world was at hand. Luke, however, rewrites the whole story of Jesus from his own distinctive point of view. He sees God's plan for the redemption of the world within a framework beginning with Creation and ending with the Second Advent. The first phase of this redemptive

[6] *Studies in the Gospels*, D. E. Nineham (ed.) (Oxford), p. 42.

history was the period of Israel, the period of the law and the prophets. The middle phase, and thus the centre of time, was the period of the ministry of Jesus, which Luke describes in his gospel.

According to Luke, says Conzelmann, 'the Good News is not that God's Kingdom has come near, but that the life of Jesus provides the foundation for the hope of the future Kingdom. Thus the nearness of the Kingdom has become a secondary factor'.[7] So God's plan of salvation passes into its third phase, the period of the Church, equipped with the Spirit and charged with the task of evangelising the world. There is no suggestion by Luke that the task will be a short one, but this final phase, this last age in which the Church now lives and works, will end with the Parousia. In the long story of the Church no period is of more significance than its beginning, the time of the first witnesses, and it is to this unique chapter of Church history that Luke devotes his second volume, *The Acts of the Apostles.*

Conzelmann has subsequently written a short commentary on the book of *Acts*[8] in which he develops this view of Luke as one of the creative theologians of the New Testament, and his approach has been supported by Ernst Haenchen in his massive commentary on *Acts*, first published in 1956.[9] For Haenchen the book of *Acts* is not a straightforward account of the apostolic age written by a contemporary, but a work of art written for

[7] (London), p. 37.
[8] *Die Apostelgeschichte* (Tübingen, 1963).
[9] *Die Apostelgeschichte* (Göttingen).

the edification of the Church in his own day towards the end of the first century by a theologically-minded author who manipulates the facts of history to serve his own purposes.

A further stage in the metamorphosis of 'Luke the historian' into 'Luke the theologian' was reached with the publication of J. C. O'Neill's study of *The Theology of Acts* in 1961. O'Neill sees Luke not as the companion of St. Paul but as an apologist of the second century, writing somewhere between A.D. 115 and 130, whose closest kinship is with Justin Martyr. 'He was,' says O'Neill, 'one of the fore-runners of the so-called "catholic" period in the history of Christian thought ... *Acts* is not primarily a history of Christian missions ... [for] Luke's primary aim was to preach the gospel to unbelievers ... Luke believed that God had prepared the Church to receive the educated and the politically powerful as well as the poor and the outcast, and he wrote *Luke–Acts* to persuade men at the centre of power to abandon their lives to the service of the kingdom of God.'[10]

Then, in 1964, came M. G. Goulder's stimulating treatment of *Acts* from the angle of typology, which he calls *Type and History in Acts*. Goulder was a pupil of Austin Farrer and his approach to *Acts* reflects Farrer's way of handling the gospels.[11] Unlike O'Neill, Goulder accepts the traditional view of the author as Paul's companion, but he credits him with having the same

[10] (London), pp. 166, 170, 173, 177.
[11] A. M. Farrer, *A Study in St. Mark* (London, 1951); *St. Matthew and St. Mark* (London, 1954).

kind of theological ingenuity as Farrer found in Mark. *Acts* is not straightforward history but a story that is told in cycles, a spiral construction which repeats the basic pattern of the Death and Resurrection of Jesus in the lives of the apostles. 'The story of *Acts* is a re-enactment of the story of the Gospel.'[12]

'The whole of *Acts*, the life of the Church,' says Goulder, 'is a reliving of Christ's life, beginning from the greatest outpouring of the Spirit at Pentecost, and ending with the greatest passion in the tribulations of Paul.'[13] Not only do we find that Luke has made events in his narrative in *Acts* correspond with types of the same kind which occur in the life of Jesus but also that he has constructed his book with an eye on the Old Testament as well. It is not just that *Acts* reveals the fulfilment of isolated passages of scripture, there is also an ordered fulfilment of the substance of the Torah, so that from the Ascension onwards the pattern of events in the new Israel points backwards to events in the lives of Abraham and Moses, and even beyond the Penta-teuch typological motifs connect up *Acts* with Joshua and the prophets.

When we ask whether in view of all this *Acts* can be taken in any sense as historical, Goulder replies with two criteria: 'Where there are no types, *Acts* is in-tended to be factual' and 'the thicker the types, the less likely is the passage to be factual'.[14] Each story in *Acts* must therefore be looked at separately. Events such as the Ascension and Pentecost will be found to be so full of typology that they must be regarded as unhistorical,

[12] *Op. cit.* (London), p. 52.   [13] p. 100.   [14] pp. 181–2.

whereas the narratives dealing with Paul's travels may be taken as containing the minimum of symbolism.

Luke, then, according to Goulder, was more of a mythographer than a theologian. He 'was both a fundamentalist and a poet, and ... he did not realise that there was any contradiction between the two ... He knows ... that he is writing what ought to have happened, as well as what must have happened and what did happen ... And as he wrote, his method made plain to him subconsciously that he was selecting, taking a sentence from this type and a phrase from that, writing an account of an ideal incident, the birth, or the Ascension of the Saviour, or the coming of his Spirit. And it was in this gift that he excelled. It is the myths of St. Luke which dominate the Christian calendar.'[15]

From 'Luke the historian' to 'Luke the theologian', and 'Luke the mythographer'—we have indeed travelled far since 1950. Whatever he turns out to be there can surely be no more inept description of him than 'the dim-wit among the evangelists' as one modern critic has called him.[16] But can he be any more properly dismissed as 'this falsifier of the Gospel' as another scholar has recently suggested?[17] Certainly the four writers whom we have been considering—Conzelmann, Haenchen, O'Neill and Goulder—however much they disagree among themselves would not ascribe to Luke the title of 'historian' in any normally accepted sense of

[15] *Op. cit.*, pp. 204–5.
[16] See footnote, p. 101, in R. H. Fuller, *The New Testament in Current Study* (London, 1963).
[17] Quoted in S. Neill, *op. cit.*, p. 265.

the word and decidedly not as it was used by Ramsay, Harnack, Streeter and Knox.

There is much indeed in the recent emphasis on 'Luke the theologian' which is open to criticism. Few of us, for example, would accept Conzelmann's thesis that in his gospel Luke's geographical references are not intended to convey information about what happened. They are always symbolic and theological. Mountain, lake, desert and plain are no more than stage-props in the story. They are introduced not because the events with which they are associated took place there but because certain types of Jesus' activity required these particular settings to indicate their significance. Similarly specific localities such as Jerusalem, Samaria and Galilee are not to be taken at their face value. They too are intended to be theologically allusive. As Goulder says, 'In his [Conzelmann's] view, St. Luke was as ignorant of the geography of Palestine as a medieval cartographer was of the land of Cathay.'[18] On the evidence of the book of *Acts* this characterisation of Luke as a geographical ignoramus is simply absurd.

By the same token, Haenchen, in his large commentary on *Acts*, tends to dismiss Luke's historical data in much too cavalier a fashion. In order to establish the author as first and foremost a theologian who wrote to edify his readers, Haenchen repeatedly does less than justice to Luke's factual information. It is not necessary to categorise a biblical narrative as unhistorical because it does not correspond with twentieth-century ideas of how history should be written, nor, when there are

[18] *Op. cit.*, pp. 142–3.

other possible explanations of an event, is it essential always to maintain that it must be an invention of the author.

Despite much that is stimulating in O'Neill's study of *The Theology of Acts*, it is unlikely that he will get much support for his argument that Luke was a second-century apologist akin to Justin Martyr. The fact that both of them bracket the gospel events with the world mission of the apostles is not conclusive, nor is O'Neill's argument that both Luke and Justin must have used a common source. John Knox in an earlier work called *Marcion and the New Testament*[19] had proposed an even later date for the finished work *Luke–Acts*, placing it about the middle of the second century, but on the whole both the protagonists of 'Luke the historian' and 'Luke the theologian' would place him firmly within the first century.

Similarly, Goulder's fascinating excursion into *Type and History in Acts* is vitiated by an excess of enthusiasm for pan-typology. When typologists get started on the New Testament there is no stopping them. Obviously the Old Testament was much in the minds of all New Testament writers and they could not fail to see the recurrent patterns which make the Bible one book and not two. Likewise it is equally obvious that the author of *Acts* saw in the early history of the Church and in the lives of the apostles a re-enactment of gospel motifs. But it is one thing to say this and quite another to claim as Goulder does, for example, that Paul breaks out of Damascus 'through the walls' (albeit in a basket)

[19] (Chicago, 1942).

'as Jesus had broken through the wall of the tomb', or that Aeneas was raised by Peter in the eighth year of his paralysis 'as Jesus had been raised on the eighth day of the week'.[20]

I have chosen these four representatives of the new picture of Luke as a theologian—Conzelmann, Haenchen. O'Neill and Goulder—because together, despite the queries we may address to this or that aspect of their case, they do seem to suggest that a reconsideration of the traditional view of the author of *Acts* as 'Luke the historian' is called for. If we accept their general position, as I think we must, that Luke was much more of a theologian than was previously thought to be the case, the next question we must ask is whether he can in any sense still be regarded as a reliable recorder of the events of the apostolic age.

[20] *Op. cit.*, pp. 95–6.

II. THE AUTHOR AND HIS PURPOSE

IT would be difficult to ignore the arguments we have been considering which are representative of a larger body of scholarly opinion. To the names of Evans, Conzelmann, Haenchen, O'Neill and Goulder we might add those of Vielhauer, Käsemann, Wilckens and others who in the last fifteen years or so have been giving the author of *Acts* a new look. As we saw, from a variety of angles modern scholars have been recasting Luke in a hitherto unfamiliar mould, that of a theologian in his own right, far removed from the traditional picture of an unpretentious missionary doctor who accompanied St. Paul on his journeys and afterwards wrote an account of them, prefacing this with what information he could pick up about the earlier stages of the birth and growth of the Church.

The question that concerns us now is whether 'Luke the theologian' leaves any room for 'Luke the historian', whether a writer who has been bold enough to put his own interpretation on the relationship between Christ and His Church can still be regarded as a reliable guide to the first thirty years of the Church's history. Right at the outset we should have to say, of course, that the historicity of the book of *Acts* does not depend on whether it was written by a companion of St. Paul or not. Sir William Ramsay, who did so much to establish the factual accuracy of *Acts*, latterly made this almost an obsession. 'It may, of course,' he said, 'be taken for granted that if Luke [i.e. the companion of Paul] did not write the *Acts*, it could not possibly be accepted [as trustworthy]. The case for belief rests on his personality.'[1]

This is an exaggeration. As we have noted, we expect of an author of a canonical New Testament book that he should be a man of God, and that he should write honestly, but if his information is defective or if he has some distinctive point of view which he is determined to put across, we shall exercise our right to have reservations about accepting his work at face value. In the case of the author of *Acts* we have already seen that there is good reason to believe that he has a theological slant, which will inevitably come between him and the events which he is recording. But what are we to say of the materials which were at the author's disposal for constructing a reliable history of the first three decades of the Christian Church?

The historicity of *Acts* depends on a variety of factors. One is certainly the material at the author's command, whether it was hearsay, or written sources, or his own experience. But another factor is how the author handles such materials as were available to him, for apart altogether from his intentional adaptation of his material in accordance with any theological purpose he may have had in mind, there is also the fact that he

[1] Quoted in Cadbury, *The Making of Luke–Acts* (New York, 1927), p. 361.

was a man of his times and could not step outside of the prevailing way of recording or interpreting such events as he had to describe. There is also to be taken into account the author's own character. For example, was Luke the sort of man who was capable of being objective?

In view of these considerations we should have to query Ramsay's dictum and say that it would be no guarantee of the historical accuracy of *Acts* even if we were able to prove beyond a shadow of doubt that the writer was the companion of Paul and had been an eye-witness of much of what he describes. As Alan Richardson has been reminding us in his recent Bampton lectures, it is not the case that 'earlier histories are more "reliable" than later ones' or that 'these sources will somehow bring us closer to "the facts" '.[2] A second-hand report might be more reliable than a first-hand one, depending on the nature of the reporter.

Nevertheless, if the evidence of *Acts* indicates that the author had an accurate knowledge of the political situation in the period he is describing, if his account of legal procedure in the course of his narrative turns out to be in accordance with the judicial practices of the time, if his geographical references are detailed and factual in those parts of his story where it appears that he himself was involved, and if what he tells us about St. Paul's missionary campaigns can be seen to tally with what the apostle himself tells us in his letters, there would seem to be a reasonable probability that the traditional view of the author as the companion

[2] *History, Sacred and Profane* (London, 1964), p. 235.

of Paul is the correct one, and that by and large we have in the book of *Acts* an invaluable and trustworthy guide to these all-important first thirty years of Church history.

The cautionary words 'by and large' are necessary in view of what has already been said about the limitations of any ancient historical writing. We are not dealing with an author who claims to be infallible. It would be natural to expect that such events as the author took part in would convey a greater sense of first-hand and accurate reporting than other events which came to the writer at second or third hand. We shall not lose faith in our author's general trustworthiness if it transpires that he occasionally gets his facts mixed up, or if his attitude to some features of his story is that of a first-century, and not a twentieth-century, recorder.

Students of the New Testament have constantly to remind themselves that recent scholarship does not necessarily mean better scholarship. As we know only too well there are trends and fashions in biblical studies as well as in other theological disciplines, and there is always the danger that in a desire to be up-to-date and 'with it' we neglect important and established findings of a past generation. Too little attention, for example, is paid by the modern exponents of the thesis that Luke was first and foremost a theologian to the work of Sir William Ramsay. As is generally recognised, Ramsay latterly went to extremes in his desire to prove by archaeology that the New Testament was accurate in every detail. But in his heyday he did on the basis of his own study of inscriptions in Asia Minor reach certain conclusions about the book of *Acts* which are still relevant.

Ramsay was convinced that the writer of *Acts* knew the world of St. Paul in the intimate way that could only have come from first-hand knowledge. Particularly is this evident in his use of official titles, which in the days of the Roman Empire, as in our own day, were a peculiarly tricky problem. When is a Mayor a Lord Mayor and when did the last Colonial Secretary stop being a Colonial Secretary? But, says Ramsay, 'the officials with whom Paul and his companions were brought in contact are those who would be there. Every person is found just where he ought to be: proconsuls in senatorial provinces, asiarchs in Ephesus, strategoi in Philippi, politarchs in Thessalonica, magicians and soothsayers everywhere.'[3]

This sort of argument does not of course prove that Luke was there, but it does suggest a writer who took care to get his facts right and who might well have been on the spot himself. One of the merits of F. F. Bruce's commentary on *Acts*[4] is that unlike some other recent writers he recognises the importance of Ramsay's findings for a general estimate of Luke's accuracy as a historian. Another contribution from an older generation which is still worthy of respect is the essay of James Smith of Jordanhill on *The Voyage and Shipwreck of St. Paul*, published in 1848, in which he argued that this particular section of *Acts* must have been written by an eye-witness who was not himself a sailor. It seems more likely that the eye-witness was the author of *Acts* him-

[3] Quoted by S. Neill, *op. cit.*, p. 143.   [4] London, 1951.

self, rather than the view canvassed by Conzelmann and others that Luke found somewhere a good story of a voyage to Rome including a shipwreck and inserted into it a few references to St. Paul.

It is surely also not without significance, as H. J. Cadbury has pointed out, that the writer of *Acts* is interested in the geographical details of Paul's journeys. He refers to Perga as being in Pamphylia, Antioch as Pisidian, Lystra and Derbe as cities of Lycaonia. Philippi is the leading city of part of Macedonia and a colony, Tarsus is in Cilicia, Myra in Lycia. He speaks of 'a certain place called Fair Havens in Crete near the town of Lasea' and of 'Phoenix, a Cretan harbour exposed south-west and north-west'. He notes the addresses of the people in his story and the places where the missionaries find lodgings: at Philippi Paul stays with Lydia, in Thessalonica with Jason, in Corinth with Aquila and Priscilla. He leaves their home and goes to lodge with Justus, whose house was next-door to the synagogue. In Joppa, Peter stays with a tanner by name Simon, whose house was by the sea.[5] Now of course the author of *Acts* may have found all these details and many more like them in some written documents which came into his hands long after the events he is recording. It is surely at least equally possible that he mentions these things because he had a good memory for what he himself had seen or heard. In either case it is difficult to understand why an author whose sole concern was theological instruction should have bothered to include such trifling matters.

[5] Cadbury, *op. cit.*, pp. 241–52.

In his recent Sarum lectures on *Roman Society and Roman Law in the New Testament* published in 1963, A. N. Sherwin-White, Reader in Ancient History at Oxford, has shed new and interesting light on our problem from the angle of classical studies. He shows that the author of *Acts* was well versed in the intricacies of Roman law as it was practised in the provinces in the middle of the first century. In the case of Paul's trials before Felix, Festus and Gallio the procedure is accurately described. On the question of the legal position of Roman citizens, Sherwin-White maintains that '*Acts* gets things right both at the general level, in its overall attitude and in specific aspects'. He concludes that in *Acts* 'the confirmation of historicity is overwhelming . . . [and] . . . any attempt to reject its basic historicity even in matters of detail must now appear absurd'. He adds that Roman historians have long taken this for granted.[6]

We shall be considering in the next lecture how far the picture of St. Paul that emerges from the pages of the book of *Acts* squares in general and in detail with the evidence of Paul's letters. I believe it can be shown that there is no real discrepancy. But even without this additional consideration there does seem to be good reason to hesitate before substituting the new image of 'Luke the theologian' for the older image of 'Luke the historian'. That he was much more of a creative theologian than was at one time thought to be the case would seem to be established, but it would seem to be equally clear that, whoever he was, the author of *Acts*

[6] *Op. cit.*, pp. 173, 189.

was extremely well informed about the political and legal institutions of the first century A.D., that he had a wide-ranging knowledge of the Mediterranean world and that his meticulous recording of detail in matters which we can verify would lead us to believe that in other matters, on which we have only his evidence, we are dealing with a recorder on whom we can rely.

If this is so, the dichotomy between 'Luke the historian' and 'Luke the theologian' is a false one, for the author of *Acts* emerges rather as a theologically-minded historian or a historically-minded theologian. In either case his narrative reveals him as being concerned with both theology and history. But who was this historical theologian or theological historian? Who was this man who shows every sign of setting the events he records in a distinctive theological framework and at the same time makes it plain that it is historical events he is relating? Was he the Luke of ancient tradition, the Gentile doctor who accompanied St. Paul on his journeys, or was he an unknown writer at the end of the first century or even in the first half of the second century who had no direct knowledge of the events he was describing?

Despite the various caveats which we have already noticed, forbidding us to assume that someone who lived closer to the period he is recording will necessarily be a more reliable reporter than someone writing at a later date, I imagine that most of us are old-fashioned enough to feel that we should have more confidence in the narrative of *Acts* if we could be reasonably certain that the author was in one way or another in close contact with the people and places that feature in his story. In the same way the value of Mark's gospel is enhanced for most of us if it can be established that behind it is the authority of St. Peter, and the fourth gospel has an added significance if we can be assured that in the background stands John the son of Zebedee.

Tradition going back to about A.D. 180 identifies the author of *Acts* as Luke, a Syrian of Antioch, a doctor by profession who had been a disciple of the apostles and had accompanied Paul until the latter's martyrdom. He is said to have died in Boeotia, unmarried, at the age of eighty-four, and to have written the third gospel and later *The Acts of the Apostles*.[7] Gallons of ink and reams of paper have been expended on demolishing this traditional view. It has been argued that our author could not have been a native of Antioch or even a Gentile. His alleged medical vocabulary indicates that he was as likely to have been a horse-doctor as a physician. He could not have been Paul's companion because he never regards Paul as an apostle on the same level as the Twelve, and if he was the writer of *Acts* he was a different man from the writer of the third gospel. We are almost left in the position of W. L. Knox's schoolboy who was being introduced to the Homeric question and said that so far as he could see it had been established that Homer was not written by Homer but by another man with the same name.[8] The only item in

[7] C. S. C. Williams, *Commentary on the Acts of the Apostles*, (London, 1957), p. 1.

[8] W. L. Knox, *The Acts of the Apostles* (Cambridge, 1948), p. 15.

the traditional picture of Luke that does not seem to have been challenged is that he died at the age of eighty-four. Perhaps this is because so many New Testament experts past and present are still themselves going strong in their eighties.

Many of the scholarly arguments in this as in all other fields of New Testament criticism cancel each other out, and here as elsewhere we cannot expect cast-iron certainties but must be content with reasonable probabilities. The traditional view has not been conclusively proved to be wrong and many of us would prefer to give more weight to early Church tradition than to the hypotheses of individual scholars. The reliability of the book of *Acts* does not in the last resort depend on whether its author came from Antioch or Macedonia, or whether he was a Gentile or a Hellenistic Jew, or whether he was the 'beloved physician' of Paul's letters. Nor, if his information was sound, does he necessarily need to have been Paul's companion on his journeys.

But if we read the book of *Acts* as dispassionately as we are able, it is difficult not to come to the conclusion that it was written by a man who not only knew what he was talking about but also was describing events in many of which he himself had taken part. Ultimately every teacher of the New Testament must speak from his own convictions and I can only say that after more than twenty years of study, teaching and discussion of the book of *Acts* I am more and more certain that when I read this fascinating account of the first three decades of the Church's history I am reading not only a masterly study by a theologically-minded historian, but also a vivid piece of first-hand reporting by someone who had been himself deeply involved in the events he describes.

When in the course of his narrative the author, whom we may as well call Luke as anything else, changes from using the word 'they' to using the word 'we', and when at these points in his story the record acquires additional realism and shows greater attention to detail, it seems to me to be sheer perversity to fail to draw the obvious conclusion. To say that this is simply an attempt on the part of the author to hoodwink his readers into the belief that he had himself been on the spot, or that it is a literary device for which parallels can be found in pagan literature, or that the 'we-passages' have been inserted into the narrative from a different source is surely to try to go to Birmingham by way of Beachy Head.

Taken at its face value, the book of *Acts* squares admirably with the traditional picture of the author as a member of St. Paul's missionary team. On the evidence of the 'we-passages', he joined the apostle halfway through his second journey, at Troas, was left behind at Philippi to follow up the work of the initial campaign there, rejoined the apostle a few years later as one of the delegates of the younger churches entrusted with conveying funds for the relief of the mother-church in Jerusalem, and from that point Luke was with Paul through his arrest in Jerusalem, his imprisonment in Caesarea and his last voyage to Rome.

Luke enters the stage about halfway through the

book of *Acts*. From then on he was either himself
present during the events that the narrative describes or
he was close enough to them through his association
with Paul and other missionaries to have a pretty good
idea of what was going on in the Church at large. For
the first half of his book, which tells the story of the
birth of the Church in Jerusalem and how it spread
through Palestine to Antioch in Syria, which became
the great new centre of Gentile Christianity, and where
Paul established his headquarters, Luke could gather
information from his many missionary contacts: Paul
himself, Philip the evangelist, doubtless some of the
Twelve Apostles, perhaps John Mark. And, being the
kind of man his book shows him to be, Luke would
make good use of his time in Caesarea where he had
two years at liberty while Paul was in prison.

Under the influence of Harnack, scholars in the first
decades of this century exercised their ingenuity in
identifying written sources which Luke was alleged to
have used in composing the early part of his book,
which covers the story of the Church before he himself
came on the scene. Largely as a result of the work of
Martin Dibelius whose highly important essays on *Acts*
began to appear in Germany in 1923, and have been
collected and published posthumously under the title, in
the English translation, of *Studies in the Acts of the
Apostles* (London, 1956), this quest for written sources
has mostly been abandoned. It was Dibelius who first
established a case for Luke as a creative author who
himself shaped the first part of his story from the

information that was available to him, rather than as a literary editor compiling documents which had been used before.

As for the second part of the book, we may leave the question open whether Luke made notes as he went along in some sort of travel-diary, or whether he amplified some kind of itinerary of Paul's journeys which covered episodes in the missionary enterprise when Luke himself was not present. If we speak in terms of a travel-diary we have still to get round A. D. Nock's awkward query as to what happened to it when the ship was wrecked on Malta. These were the days before plastic containers, but perhaps they had other methods.

After a searching examination of the whole subject the most recent writer on *The Sources of Acts*, the Roman Catholic scholar Jacques Dupont in a book which bears that title, published in English in 1964, recognises that it is impossible 'to define any of the sources used by the author of *Acts* in a way which will meet with widespread agreement among the critics'. He comes to the conclusion, which he shares with Père Benoit, that the book of *Acts* was written in stages and that it is 'based not on sources coming from another author, but on Luke's own notes'.[9]

Scholars of Harnack's generation set out on the quest for the sources that lie behind *Acts* on the assumption that Luke must have used the same methods in composing *Acts* as he has used in composing his gospel, where he combines Mark, Q and his own special material. This

[9] (London), pp. 166–7.

newer view that in the case of *Acts* it was all his own
material that he was using, and that it went through
several stages of editing and re-editing by the author
himself, would account for some of the features of the
book that seem to suggest pre-existing sources. There
may be a lesson for us in a comparable case in classical
philology: 'About a hundred years ago the German
scholar Otto Ribbeck conjectured that half a dozen of
the later satires were not by Juvenal at all but by a
forger who copied something of his manner without
equalling his spirit. He was right, but the copyist was
Juvenal himself, imitating his earlier work after the
passion that inspired it had died away.'[10]

We seem then to see a more complete picture of Luke
emerging from all this: a theologically-minded historian who is also an author in his own right, the
creator of a book which has a unique place in the New
Testament and which deals with a unique period of
Church history. There is no certainty about where or
when he wrote it. Perhaps it was in Rome, perhaps in
Greece, and probably in the seventies or eighties of the
first century. Dibelius makes the point that Luke's name
must have been attached to both his volumes from the
beginning. He suggests that it is most unlikely that two
books dedicated to a named patron, in this case Theophilus, could have been sold to educated readers in the
bookshops of the day without the author's name being
known. He surmises that they may have appeared

[10] Gilbert Highet, *Juvenal the Satirist* (Oxford, 1954), pp. 4-5,
quoted by R. M. Grant, *A Historical Introduction to the New
Testament* (London, 1963), p. 215.

under the titles of *Luke's Acts of Jesus* and *Luke's Acts of the Apostles*.

But why did *Acts* appear at all? What was Luke's purpose in writing it? First of all let us remember that we are talking about Part II of a two-volume work. Few scholars, ancient or modern, have dissented from this view. But for the fact that in the traditional arrangement of the New Testament writings the fourth gospel comes between the two parts of Luke's work, this point would hardly need emphasising. It does help to remind us, however, that this theologically-minded historian is primarily an evangelist. Whatever other motives our author may have had in mind in writing this literary masterpiece his fundamental object was to proclaim the good news. The book of *Acts* like the third gospel tells the story of what God has done for the world through Jesus, and the main clue to our understanding of what made Luke write them both is that, as Harnack said, he was an 'enthusiast for Christ'.

Little support is now given to Streeter's view that Luke wrote his two volumes to serve as a legal brief for Theophilus, charged with the task of defending St. Paul on trial for his life in Rome. The only advantage of this theory would seem to be that it solves the problem of why the book of *Acts* ends where it does, with Paul in prison, awaiting trial, without going on to tell us the outcome. We shall have to look at this point more closely later. But there is so much in both the gospel and *Acts* that would be quite irrelevant for any advocate preparing a speech for the apostle's defence that this particular suggestion appears to be quite inadequate to cover the facts.

Dibelius draws a distinction between the readers for whom the gospel was designed and those whom Luke had in mind when he wrote *Acts*. The gospel, says Dibelius, was written for the Church but *Acts* was written for the world. It was written for the book-market, for private reading by educated pagans.[11] O'Neill similarly claims that in *Acts* Luke is preaching the gospel primarily for unbelievers.[12] But it seems unnecessary to limit Luke's purpose in this way. Surely he is writing both for the Church and the world, and above all for the Church in the world. He is thinking not only of intelligent enquirers outside the Church who want to know what Christianity is all about, but for intelligent enquirers inside the Church who want to know how it all began.

Luke's work has sometimes been called an *apologia* for Christianity. But this again is to limit its scope. He is not primarily defending the faith, he is proclaiming it. And it is here that the more recent emphasis on Luke as a theologian finds its place. What makes his two-volume work unique in the New Testament is that he does something that no other evangelist and no letter-writer, even St. Paul, attempts to do. Mark in his gospel tells of the redemptive acts of God in the life, death and Resurrection of Jesus. His gospel ends on a note of expectancy. The Lord will come again in glory and the time will not be long. For St. Paul the story of redemption begins where Mark leaves off. He has little to say of

[11] *Op. cit.*, p. 148.   [12] *Op. cit.*, p. 173.

the ministry of Jesus, for in his mind it was but the prelude to His death and Resurrection which ushered in the new age, where the risen and glorified Christ is present with His people through His Spirit.

Thus, as C. K. Barrett points out, Mark only hints at the future life of the Church and Paul only hints at the historical Jesus. Neither of them deals with the relationship between the Jesus of history and the Church. But this is precisely what Luke does. In his two-volume work he builds a bridge between the two. It is thus not without significance that he tells the story of the Ascension twice: once at the end of his gospel and again at the beginning of *Acts*.

In Luke's mind the Ascension of Christ has two aspects. In the gospel it is the end of the story of Jesus, in *Acts* it is the beginning of the story of the Church, which will go on until Christ comes again. Thus for Luke, as Barrett says, 'the end of the story of Jesus is the Church, and the story of Jesus is the beginning of the Church'. For Mark and Paul Jesus is the End— God's last word. With this Luke agrees, but for him Jesus is also the beginning of something else. In one way or another the whole of the New Testament sees the time after the Resurrection as the last chapter in history. For Luke, however, the last chapter is a new chapter, and Christ 'is not the close of all history, but the starting point of a new kind of history, Church History'. Luke is thus entitled, Barrett concludes, to be called 'the Father of Church History', since no one before his day had realised that there was such a thing, and no one else in the New Testament had the same

vision of something that had just begun but whose end
was on the far horizon.[13]

But Luke's Church history in *Acts* is no mere recital
of what happened in these early decades. It is history
written by a theologian and a preacher. Luke is convinced that God's redemption of the world and renewal
of its life continues through the work of His servants in
the Church. There is nothing casual or accidental in
its growth and progress. The hand of God is in everything that happens; the Church advances irresistibly in
the power of the Spirit. God's plan for the salvation of
the world which began through Israel and was crystal-
lised in the life, death and Resurrection of Jesus, pro-
ceeds on its victorious way to its appointed end despite
all obstacles and human perversity.

So M. G. Goulder is right to urge us to see in the
pageant of *Acts* a re-enactment of the gospel story and
of the great themes of Old Testament redemptive history. How could Luke have written otherwise when he
saw in his mind's eye the whole majestic sweep of God's
dealings with man from the Creation to the Parousia?
In this great panorama he concentrates on one tiny
period of thirty years, three short decades, but how
critical they are for the Church and the world. His
version of the gospel traces the descent of Jesus back to
Adam, the type of mankind. The story he tells in *Acts*
leads us from Jerusalem to Rome, the heart of civilisa-
tion as Luke knew it, the symbol of the world as it is,
and of man in need of salvation.

[13] For the substance of these last two paragraphs I am indebted
to C. K. Barrett, *op. cit.*, pp. 53–8.

Streeter suggested that an alternative title for the book of *Acts* might be 'The Road to Rome', for this is indeed the significance of Luke's work. If these lectures had not been delivered in the proximity of John Knox's statue and in the present ecumenical climate I should have called this series just that, rather than borrow a title from G. B. Caird's admirable textbook. For whatever minor motifs Luke had in mind, such as the establishment of Christianity in men's minds as a constructive and not destructive element in the social order, his main concern was to show that in God's plan for the renewal of the life of mankind Jerusalem, the heart of old Israel, was the goal of Stage One, while Rome, the centre of the world, was the goal of Stage Two. From there the future lay open, and time would not be reckoned in decades but, for all Luke knew, in centuries and millennia. Meanwhile, however, his task was to recall the foundation and first definitive period of the Church. The acts of the Twelve Apostles and above all of the thirteenth apostle St. Paul were basic to the whole enterprise of the evangelisation of mankind, and it is to this that we shall next turn.

III. PAUL AND THE TWELVE

It has often been said by writers about the book of *Acts* that Luke made Paul his hero. Certainly the other apostles, even Peter, are given much more sketchy treatment. More than half of *Acts* is devoted to the life and work of Paul, although Luke makes it quite clear that in the expansion of the Church through the pagan world countless other Christians, named and unnamed, had a part in spreading the gospel among the Gentiles. Clearly it is not, as might at one time have been thought, the uncritical hero-worship of a simple medical missionary. Not only does Luke paint his picture of Paul with 'warts and all', but, as we have seen, our author is a man of independent judgment with a theological point of view of his own. In underlining the significance of Paul's contribution so heavily he must have had a better reason than admiration of Paul as a tireless and intrepid adventurer for Christ.

A possible explanation might be found in the new characterisation of Paul which was suggested by Johannes Munck of Aarhus in his book *Paul and the Salvation of Mankind* published in 1959.[1] Munck's argument is that Paul conceived himself to be in a special way a key figure in God's purpose of salvation.

[1] E.T., London.

His conversion was not the explosion of his growing uneasiness about the claims of Judaism, or the direct result of Stephen's martyrdom, but a call, such as came to Moses or Jeremiah, to play the supreme role in the unfolding drama of the impending end of the world. Christ had appeared, the consummation was at hand, and it was to be Paul's mission to bring it about. By confronting the Gentiles in the East and in the West with the gospel, he would personally achieve their representative salvation. When East and West had thus been saved in principle, the Jews would be moved to turn to Christ and the time for the Parousia would have come through the work of God's appointed agent.

In support of his case Munck adduces II *Thessalonians* 2 : 6–7 among other pieces of evidence. This, you will remember, is that most obscure of all New Testament passages about the delay of the Parousia, the activities of the Man of Sin, and the power that restrains him. If this passage can be made to mean anything at all it is usually interpreted in terms of the Roman Empire and the Emperor, or in terms of apocalyptic imagery. Munck, however, maintains that Paul is talking about himself. *He* is the power that restrains the Man of Sin, and his preaching of the gospel stands between the world and the Parousia. When Paul has fulfilled his representative task of evangelising the Gentiles, the Man of Sin will appear and be destroyed as a prelude to the appearance of Christ. In this interpretation of the difficult passage in *Thessalonians* Munck agrees with Oscar Cullmann who had ventilated the same idea in an article as far back as 1936[2], but I cannot myself believe that this is what the apostle meant.

Munck goes on to deny that there was any real conflict between Paul and the Jerusalem Christians. The early Church was of one mind, he says, on the need to evangelise the Gentiles. What troubles they encountered came not from a pro-Jewish faction within the Christian communities but from Judaising Gentiles. This view seems to run so counter to what appears to be the plain evidence of the New Testament as to merit the charge of special pleading. But more important is surely the weakness in Munck's case which almost turns the apostle into a megalomaniac. Undoubtedly he was a totally dedicated missionary and Luke thought of him as the greatest of the apostles—but surely Paul never thought of himself as the only apostle who mattered, the pivot round which the whole plan of salvation revolved. The Paul whom we encounter in the book of *Acts* as well as in his own letters was far too conscious of the significance of the whole Church as the Body of Christ to think of himself as a kind of eschatological one-man band.

If it is not for this reason that Luke makes Paul his hero, it is equally not because our author was a devotee of Pauline theology. He does not distinguish Paul's characteristic view of salvation from that of the other apostles. Justification by faith is mentioned but no more (13:39) and the significance of the death of Christ plays little part in Luke's summaries of Paul's preaching. Luke does not regard it as a peculiarly Pauline

[2] *Revue d'Histoire et de Philosophie Religieuse*, p. 210 f.

emphasis that circumcision should not be obligatory for Gentiles, and on the other hand he goes out of his way to point out that Paul regarded observance of the Law as incumbent upon Jews.

It has often been pointed out that Paul might not have written any of the epistles whatever for all the notice Luke takes of them, and of the theological ideas expressed in them. Even allowing for the fact that Paul's letters do not seem to have been generally known much before the end of the first century, one would think that if Luke wrote *Acts* in Rome at any time after Paul's death he would have at least known the contents of the letter to the Romans, or, if he wrote it in Greece, one or other of the letters to Corinth or Philippi or Thessalonica must have come his way.

The most likely explanation of this neglect is that Luke was not particularly interested in Paul as an individualistic theologian. But then neither was the Church in general in the seventies or eighties of the first century. Perhaps Luke was an early exponent of the view later expressed by the writer of II *Peter* that in the epistles of our beloved brother Paul there are some things hard to understand (II *Pet.* 3:16). More likely Luke, like others in the early Church, honoured Paul for more practical reasons. He saw him as one of the great martyrs of the young Church, who had preached the gospel and witnessed to his faith and given his life for his Master in the heart of the Empire, but more than that he honoured him because he had brought the message of salvation from Jerusalem to Rome.

This was why Luke made Paul his hero, if we like to

put it that way. In fulfilment of Old Testament prophecy Jesus had come to bring light into the darkness of
the Gentile world. From Pentecost onwards His Spirit
had driven His followers, Peter above all, to recognise
that their task was to be His witnesses 'in Jerusalem and
in all Judaea, and in Samaria and unto the uttermost
part of the earth' (1:8). This was the succession in
which Paul stood and none of the other apostles had
done more to make this mission to the Gentiles a
reality. When Paul reached Rome, God's plan for the
salvation of the world was in principle accomplished.
However far ahead the last act in the divine drama
might lie and whatever unexpected reverses might yet
be encountered before God's purpose for the world was
effected through His Church, Luke would see to it that
no one could be in any doubt as to the mighty role that
was played under God's hand by this one-time scourge
of the saints, who became the chief architect of the
Israel of God.

It is for this reason that the book of *Acts* ends as it
does, with Paul in Rome awaiting trial, under house-
arrest but still in his confinement allowed to preach
the gospel, as Luke says, 'quite openly and without
hindrance' (28:31). The older view that Luke left the
story of Paul in mid-air because he wrote *Acts* at that
very point in time, that is, before Paul's martyrdom,
which is generally dated at A.D. 64, is difficult to sub-
stantiate nowadays. Among other things it would mean
that *Acts* was written before Mark's gospel appeared,
say in A.D. 65, and since the third gospel, the first of
Luke's two volumes, clearly depends on *Mark* for

much of its contents, *Acts* must be later than both of them.

What happened to Paul after Luke's story ends is to some extent conjectural. Was he acquitted and did he then embark on further missionary journeys, and if so was it to Spain, as Clement of Rome seems to suggest, or did he return to the East as the Pastoral Epistles imply? The answer involves us in many problems, not least the authenticity of the letters to Timothy and Titus. But, whatever preceded it, St. Paul's martyrdom in Rome at the same time as St. Peter's as a result of the Emperor Nero's victimisation of the Christians for the burning of the city in A.D. 64, is so firmly embedded in early Church tradition that we may take it as established. This fact would be so well known to the readers of *Acts* that there was no need for Luke to include it. In any event his primary aim is not to write a full-length life of the apostle but to show how God used him to bring the gospel to the nerve-centre of the pagan world. Luke ends his story of the life of Jesus with the picture of the disciples after the Ascension spending all their time in the temple at Jerusalem praising God for what they had seen and heard (*Luke* 24 : 53). He now completes the sequel to this story with the picture of Christ's greatest disciple, after surviving countless hazards and surmounting gargantuan obstacles, installed by God's invincible purpose in the heart of the Roman empire, proclaiming the Good News of man's salvation 'without hindrance'. With this expression, which is literally Luke's last word in *Acts*, he is saying that largely through Paul's activities the Church is now on the march and nothing can stop it. Paul has built the vital bridge from Jerusalem to Rome. The Cross is in the field.

If, however, Luke had so deep a sense of the significance of Paul in the history of the Church, we may well wonder why he does not more obviously give Paul the status of apostolic authority which he accords to the Twelve, a status which if we are to judge by Paul's own letters to Galatia and Corinth he himself regarded as all-important (*Gal.* 2:8; I *Cor.* 9:1). On the Damascus road he had received a direct commission from Christ Himself and whatever views others may have taken of what that implied, Paul certainly regarded his own authority in the Church as no less than that of the Jerusalem apostles. B. S. Easton insists that Luke is determined to keep Paul in his place. While recognising him as an apostle, like Barnabas (14:14), Luke never disguises the fact that he considered his status in the Church as being inferior to that of the Twelve,[3] and Haenchen uses the same argument to deny that the author of *Acts* could possibly have been a companion of Paul. No one who knew Paul well, says Haenchen, could conceivably have failed to emphasise his claim to be an equal of St. Peter and the others.[4]

I wonder if this is so. It is difficult to think that Luke regarded Paul, to whose activities he devotes sixteen chapters of his book, as significantly inferior to Matthias, who was chosen to take the place of Judas Iscariot as one of the Twelve, but who is never even mentioned

[3] *Early Christianity*, F. C. Grant (ed.), 1954, pp. 60–2.
[4] *Op. cit.*, pp. 102–3.

again, after his election in chapter one, in the remaining twenty-seven chapters. Moreover, it is likely that by the time Luke came to write *Acts*, twenty years or so after Paul's martyrdom, the importance of the Twelve as a body compared with their associates was no longer a burning issue. They had been undoubtedly the Founding Fathers of the Church. They had served their turn as a symbol of the twelve tribes of Israel, translated into a Christian setting, worthy of respect as guarantors of the faith in the earliest days of the Church, but from Luke's point of view they had passed into history. He would not have been adding anything to his eulogy of Paul if he had asserted his right to be ranked equal with a body of men most of whom were unknown even by name to the Gentile world. What had mattered greatly to Paul thirty years earlier in his running battle with Jewish-Christian extremists who sought to discredit the apostle on the grounds that he lacked the status and authority of the original Twelve was at the time of the writing of *Acts* largely a matter of academic interest.

In this as in other respects Luke's portrait of Paul serves as a catalyst of some of the apparently contradictory impressions we get of the apostle from his letters. The relationship between *Acts* and Paul's epistles is one of mutual illumination, and while obviously the evidence of the epistles is primary, the framework provided by the book of *Acts* is invaluable. From Luke's narrative we see Paul in perspective against the skilfully delineated background of the Jewish and Gentile world, as part, albeit a major part, of the great forward movement of the Church in the first three decades of its history. Many of the battles which Paul is fighting in his letters have been won, much of the dust stirred up in his many controversies has settled. Luke, as a participant in much of Paul's story, can now look back in tranquillity and see the whole amazing drama of these early years unfolding.

The Jerusalem that Paul knew is in ruins, the old mother-church is scattered, the Jewish-Gentile controversy that bedevilled Paul's ministry has been largely solved by political developments outside the control of the Church. In all of this Luke cannot but see the hand of God. So the cause of Gentile freedom from Jewish legalism for which Paul fought so valiantly can be viewed dispassionately and seen to be part of the teething troubles of the infant Church. As we have noted, Luke is a theologian in his own right, but he is more of a churchman in his theology than a Paulinist. Judging from Luke's writings, the profundities in Paul's thinking which evoked a response in minds like those of Augustine, Luther and Barth made little impact on our author's understanding of Christianity. It is perhaps just because he is the kind of man who is not dazzled by Paul's dialectical skill and theological expertise that Luke can give us in *Acts* a picture of the apostle which not only adds much to what we learn from Paul himself in his letters but also enables us to form a truer estimate of Paul as seen through the eyes of a highly intelligent friend and fellow-worker.

When I was a student, scholars were still busy refuting the views of Reitzenstein, Bousset, Kirsopp Lake and others that St. Paul had turned Christianity into a

Greek mystery religion and had corrupted the simple Palestinian gospel of Jesus; that sacramentalism, redemption by a dying and rising Saviour, initiation by baptism, mystical union with Jesus as Kurios or Lord, all derived from Paul's Hellenisation of Christianity. There is very little if anything of this now. The whole trend in recent decades has been to emphasise the Hebrew background of Paul's thinking, as indeed the apostle himself unmistakably asserts, and as the book of *Acts* confirms. Like a good missionary he used terminology that meant more to Gentile audiences than Jewish ideas, like that of the Messiah and the Kingdom, but it was essentially the same gospel that he preached as according to Luke was preached at Pentecost. Gregory Dix's little book *Jew and Greek*[5] is an admirable exposition of this view.

A few years ago W. G. Kümmel of Marburg in his presidential address to the Society for New Testament Studies[6] took as his theme the continuity between Jesus and Paul and showed how dependent Paul was, not on extraneous Hellenistic ideas, but on Jesus Himself with his Old Testament and Palestinian background. This was despite the fact that like W. L. Knox,[7] Bultmann[8] and H. J. Schoeps,[9] Kümmel is inclined to place more

[5] London, 1953.

[6] *New Testament Studies*, Vol. 10, No. 2, 1964.

[7] *Some Hellenistic Elements in Primitive Christianity* (London, 1944).

[8] *Theology of the New Testament*, Vol. 1 (E.T., London, 1952).

[9] *Paul, the Theology of the Apostle in the Light of Jewish History* (E.T., London, 1961).

emphasis on the Greek background of Paul's thought than most modern scholars are prepared to do.

Probably the most important book on the subject—and one of the best books on Paul since the Second World War—is W. D. Davies' *Paul and Rabbinic Judaism*.[10] Davies' thesis is that although his life was dedicated to the conversion of the Gentiles, St. Paul remained a Hebrew of the Hebrews and baptised his rabbinic heritage into Christ. From another angle A. M. Hunter in *Paul and his Predecessors*[11] has shown how much the theology of St. Paul derives from the Jewish-Christian tradition which he took over at his conversion, and an interesting suggestion has come from W. C. van Unnik, in a book called *Tarsus or Jerusalem? The city of Paul's youth*,[12] that the apostle was no more than born in Tarsus but spent his boyhood and schooldays in Jerusalem.

The argument turns on what is meant by *Acts* 22:3, where St. Paul at his arrest in Jerusalem claims that he was born in Tarsus yet brought up in this city, i.e. Jerusalem, at the feet of Gamaliel. If this means what van Unnik says it means, it implies that even what little early Greek influence the apostle could hardly help absorbing in the imperial city of his boyhood must now be questioned, and he emerges as an out-and-out Jerusalem Jew until his conversion. But even if van Unnik is wrong, it has become increasingly clear of recent years that there was far less difference than was thought to be the case between Judaism as it was known in Palestine

[10] London, 1948.   [11] London, 1940.
[12] E.T., London, 1962.

in Paul's day, and Judaism as he would have known it in the Jewish colony of the Greek city of Tarsus. The Hellenisation of the ancient world had infiltrated even into the tradition of Israel, and whether Paul was brought up in Tarsus or Jerusalem there is no need to look for the sources of his ideas anywhere but in Judaism.

When we add to this the new light which is being shed on aspects of Paul's thought by the Dead Sea Scrolls, the Palestinian imprint on his thinking becomes even more pronounced. He tells us himself in his letters that he was a Pharisaic Jew of the strictest type (*Gal.* 1 : 13 f.; *Phil.* 3 : 5 f.) and this is confirmed by Luke in *Acts* (23 : 6). The further evidence of *Acts* is that after his conversion to Christianity his concern for his own kinsfolk as the legatees of God's promises and the people of the covenant persisted. It was not merely missionary strategy that took him first to the synagogues in his missionary campaigns but a deep sense that the gospel must first be preached to the Jews.

There were almost no lengths to which Paul was not prepared to go to demonstrate his respect for the Law as the divinely ordained way of life for those who bore the Jewish name. Antioch was his base of operations, but Jerusalem was his spiritual home. The Temple and its festivals—Passover and Pentecost—as well as the material needs of his Jewish-Christian brethren seem never to have been far from the forefront of his mind. On his last visit to the Holy City he accedes to the request of the Jerusalem church leaders that he should openly identify himself as a true son of the Law by associating himself in the Temple with some Jewish-Christians who had undertaken Nazirite vows (21 : 17–26), and in the last scene of all that Luke describes in *Acts* he is pressing the claims of Christianity as the fulfilment of the Law and the prophets upon the leaders of the Jewish community in Rome (28 : 17–28).

For this intensely loyal Jew had, through his shattering experience on the Damascus road, learned to see the limitations of the Law. His vision of the risen Christ brooked no denial. Jesus of Nazareth who had died a felon's death under the curse of the Law was indeed the Messiah of psalm and prophecy. The salvation of the world lay through the Cross and not through the Law of Moses. Contrary to everything he had been brought up to believe Paul was forced to acknowledge that the despised Nazarenes were the true people of God, and from this recognition it followed inevitably that the barrier that separated Jew from Gentile had been broken by what God had done in Christ. Jews and Gentiles, each following their own tradition, were now to be gathered into one household of faith, the Church which is the body of Christ. It is a striking fact that in Luke's three accounts of Paul's conversion (chs. 9, 22, 26) he focuses attention on two aspects: Paul is summoned to come into the Church and at the same time he is called to go out into the Gentile world.

It is the great merit of Luke's delineation of Paul that he shows him in the story of *Acts* not to have been an individualistic theologian, patenting his own brand of Christianity and foisting it upon the world. Rather he depicts him as a true Israelite, deeply conscious of what the Old Testament heritage meant for Christians, yet deeply conscious also of the common faith which he shared with all other Christians, and of his membership of a common fellowship into which he had been welcomed at his conversion. Of Paul's genius as an interpreter to the world at large of the 'breadth and length and height and depth of the love of Christ' (*Eph.* 3:18) Luke has little to say, for his task is rather to show Paul's greatness in action as the master-mind of the Christian mission, a Hebrew of the Hebrews who nevertheless made the Gentile world his parish.

We shall have occasion in a subsequent lecture to look more closely at the role of the Twelve Apostles as a body in the structure of the early Church as Luke describes it. Here let us try to see them as individuals. In the first few verses of his book Luke has given us the names of eleven of them: Peter, John, James, Andrew, Philip, Thomas, Bartholomew, Matthew, James the son of Alphaeus, Simon the Zealot and Judas the son of James. Then, as he tells us, to fill the vacant place of Judas Iscariot, a new apostle, Matthias, was added to complete the Twelve. As we have already seen, Matthias is never mentioned again, but astonishingly enough, neither are most of the others. Apart from Peter and John, and a mention of James by name only to record his death (12:2), as individuals the Twelve fade out of the record.

Clearly Luke regarded them as a body as highly important, but his problem when he came to write *Acts* must have been that he could find out little about them. This is perhaps not surprising. As Haenchen has pointed out,[13] the first generation of Christians was deeply interested in what Jesus had said and done, and this was what the Twelve and their successors proclaimed. What the apostles themselves had said and done only became of interest to a later generation, such as that for which Luke was writing, but there was all too little that he could find to tell. Men who were living in expectation of the end of the world and the return of Christ, as were the first generation Christians, would remember the message of the preachers rather than details about the preachers themselves.

Accordingly it is the acts of the apostles in the wider sense that Luke describes in his narrative, primarily of Paul and his associates, Barnabas, Silvanus, Timothy and the rest, for he had no lack of information about these, or of Stephen and Philip who are also part of Paul's story. But it would be true to say that, as in the novels of Sir Walter Scott, Luke's thumbnail sketches of minor characters in his book make them come alive more vividly than the more important personages in the narrative. True, we get a clear picture of Stephen as a brilliant pioneer of the more radical type of Christianity and of Barnabas as a man of great integrity, wide sympathy and much wisdom. But compared with Philip and Silvanus, for example, who played major roles in the work of the mission, little people with walking-on parts like the worthy gaoler at Philippi, Rhoda the flustered maid-of-all-work in Mary's house in Jerusalem and Demetrius the trade-union organiser in Ephesus are much more memorable.

[13] *Op. cit.*, pp. 86–7.

The picture of Paul so dominates the scene that the other apostles tend to be dwarfed. But there is one exception, and we may leave out of account for the moment James, the brother of the Lord, the *éminence grise* of the mother-church at Jerusalem whose shadow falls darkly across Paul's mission to the Gentiles and to whom we shall return later. Paul, as we know from his letter to the Galatians, regarded him as the arch-reactionary, but James was not an apostle in the sense of being a missionary. The exception to the generalisation that Luke's narrative is largely about the acts of the thirteenth apostle is of course St. Peter. It would not be far from the truth to say that what Luke describes in his book is the acts of Peter and Paul.

From the beginning of his story Luke shows Peter to have been the undoubted head of the Church, its chief spokesman and acknowledged leader. He assumes the authority which our Lord conferred on Peter at Caesarea Philippi (*Matt.* 16:16–19) and this authority is accepted by all, although Luke in his gospel, presumably without knowledge of Matthew's fuller account, follows Mark in his abbreviated version of how Peter acclaimed Jesus as the Messiah. It has never been any easier for Protestants to accept the scriptural evidence about the place of Peter in the early Church than it has been for them to do justice to the status of our Lord's Mother. Mariolatry and exaggerated papal claims have done a grave disservice to both. In the case of Peter, Protestantism has often sought to counter Catholic claims by overstressing Paul and underrating the Rock on which Jesus promised that He would build

His Church. The book of *Acts* gives us a truer perspective.

From the beginning of the Church's story Peter occupies a unique position. He it is who even before Pentecost insists that the vacant place of Judas Iscariot must be filled and who presides over the appointment of Matthias to complete the number of the Twelve Apostles. At Pentecost it is Peter who as spokesman explains to the assembled crowd the meaning of the visitation of the Holy Spirit. In the healing of the cripple at the Temple it is Peter's action which first rouses the ire of the authorities against the Nazarenes, and it is Peter again who successfully justifies what has been done in the name of Christ. The macabre tale of the notorious Ananias and Sapphira is marked by the general acceptance of Peter's disciplinary authority within the Church, and although we are told that other apostles had the gift of healing it is only of Peter that it is said that the popular estimate of his healing power was so great that even his shadow falling across a sick man was believed to be efficacious. Peter is quite clearly the head of the Church in its earliest stage (chs. 1–5).

This supremacy of Peter in the Jerusalem Church is not only attested by *Acts* but also confirmed by St. Paul. He tells us in his letter to the Galatians that on his first visit to Jerusalem three years after his conversion it was Peter he went to see (*Gal.* 1 : 18). It would seem that even then, although James, the Lord's brother, was becoming a power to be reckoned with among the Jerusalem Christians, Peter was still pre-eminent. When a more radical spirit came into the Church, under the influence of Stephen and the Hellenists, and the first persecution of the Nazarenes resulted in the beginning of missionary enterprise by the fugitives among the Samaritans, the conservative Twelve, including Peter, represented a type of Christianity which was sufficiently indistinguishable from Judaism to make it possible for them to remain unmolested in Jerusalem. Peter indeed, accompanied by John, is delegated by the Twelve to go down to Samaria and regularise the full admission of the converts there into the Church (chs. 6–8).

From then on he seems to have himself embarked on missionary activities among Jews. We hear of him at Lydda and Joppa, and it was presumably as a result of wider missionary work of this kind carried on by the Twelve that James, the Lord's brother, became head of the local church in Jerusalem. But according to Luke it was the encounter with Cornelius, the Roman centurion in Caesarea, that transformed Peter, the staunch Jewish-Christian, into the first protagonist of the mission of the Church to the Gentiles (chs. 9–10). So much is made of this incident in the book of *Acts* that it is plain, as Dibelius has pointed out,[14] that, for Luke, Cornelius is not the main character in the story, but Peter. It is not Cornelius' conversion to Christianity that matters so much as the fact that Peter is given such unmistakable indication that the gospel is for Gentiles as well as Jews. By the undoubted prompting of the Holy Spirit the head of the Church is forced to recognise the import-ance of the Gentile mission. All that we are told about Peter subsequently suggests that although he was tactic-

[14] *Op. cit.*, p. 118.

ally the leader of the Jewish-Christian mission as Paul was of the Gentile-Christian mission, 'in the entire tragic debate whose echoes we hear in all the letters of Paul'—the question as to how far Jewish practices should be incumbent upon Gentile Christians—'Peter himself,' in Cullmann's words, 'no doubt stood nearer to Paul than did the other members of the Jerusalem mission.'[15]

According to *Acts*, after his escape from prison during Herod's persecution of the Church, Peter left Jerusalem and went off to 'another place' (12 : 17). Whether Luke has any definite place in mind or whether he was simply clearing the stage for the appearance of Paul, who from this point onward is the centre of attention, is not clear. Certainly Luke sees the careers of Peter and Paul as following parallel lines and does not think of them in any sense as rivals for the leadership of the Church. According to early tradition both of them witnessed for their faith by martyrdom in Rome, so that as Cadbury says, 'even in their death they were not divided'.[16] As an associate and admirer of Paul, and because of his deep sense of the importance of the mission to the Gentiles, Luke has made Paul the hero of his story, but not at the expense of Peter, who quite clearly from the record stands out in Luke's mind as the Rock on whom the whole Church was founded.

[15] Oscar Cullmann, *Peter, Disciple—Apostle—Martyr* (London, 1953), p. 45.
[16] H. J. Cadbury, *The Book of Acts in History* (London, 1955), p. 132.

IV. THE FAITH OF THE CHURCH

As we saw in an earlier lecture it was Martin Dibelius who, so to speak, turned the tide of scholarly opinion back from the frustrating quest of sources which the author of *Acts* was supposed to have used for the earlier part of his book, covering the period before he entered the stage himself as the missionary companion of St. Paul. Dibelius has persuaded most critics that it is to Luke himself that we must turn, seeing him as author rather than editor, not a compiler who pieced together material that had been used before, but a creative historian who in the first half of his book gives us a picture of the life of the Church before the impact of St. Paul upon it, based on such information as he had been able to collect.

Now if by that Dibelius (who, unlike most of the recent German writers on the subject, believed that the author of *Acts* was actually, as tradition maintained, the doctor from Antioch who accompanied Paul on his journeys) had meant that Luke had used the ample opportunities which the book of *Acts* suggests to find out from first-hand witnesses what had happened in the Church in Jerusalem and Palestine generally before he came on the scene, we should be happy indeed to follow his lead. For we should then have an invaluable insight into the beliefs and practices of the first Christians, based on actual reminiscences of what had happened on this or that occasion and what had been the substance of the earliest Christian preaching.

But this is not at all what Dibelius meant when he called Luke the first Christian historian. He reckons that apart from some popular stories, such as those of the healing of the cripple in the Temple and the dramatic tale of Ananias and Sapphira, Luke had little to go on. He linked these few stories together, supplied himself the narrative summaries of the Church's development, and above all wrote all the speeches or sermons that are credited to Peter, Paul, Stephen and the rest out of his own head. This may indeed enhance our opinion of Luke as a literary craftsman, but it does not encourage us to turn to the book of *Acts* if we are looking for evidence of what the earliest Christians believed. For in Dibelius' view the sermons that Luke incorporates in his narrative are much more models of what he considered preaching in his own day should be like, than in any sense reflections of how the earliest apostles proclaimed the gospel.[1]

This is of course a crucial issue. It is not without value for us today to know how the message of Christianity was presented to the world in the last decades of the first century but we already have the letters of Paul which tell us how the faith was being expressed by the middle of the first century. If the book of *Acts* is to add anything to this it must be because it enables us to go further back still. We may follow Gregory Dix in divid-

[1] *Op. cit.*, pp. 123–85.

ing the history of the apostolic Church roughly into
three decades: the first, from A.D. 30 to 40, when
Christianity was still a movement within Syrian Judaism; the second decade, from A.D. 40 to 50, when the
Jewish Christian mission went out among the Jews of
the Dispersion; and the third, from A.D. 50 to 60,
when the Church leapt from the Syriac to the Greek
world.[2]

Again, speaking generally, the third decade is covered
by St. Paul's letters and to some extent by the sermons
and speeches of Paul in the second half of the book of
Acts. But it is to the first half of the book of *Acts* and
there alone that we should want to turn, to the preaching of Peter and Stephen, to find the form and substance of the Christian message as it was being proclaimed in the first two decades of the Church's history,
beginning with Pentecost and ending with the first
appearance of Paul's letters. If, as many of the most recent writers on the book of *Acts* maintain, Luke, or
whoever they think the author of *Acts* may have been,
composed himself the sermons and speeches he includes
in his history, putting them into the mouths of Peter
and Stephen, we have no grounds for believing that we
can by studying *Acts* hope to penetrate beyond St. Paul
into the thoughts of those who were Christians before
him. According to these scholars we cannot regard the
theology of *Acts* as representing the first stage of Christian belief, but merely what the author of *Acts* thought
the first Christians might have believed, or should have
believed, or how Christians in his own day several

[2] *Op. cit.*, p. 27.

decades later formulated their own faith or in the author's view ought to formulate it.

I confess that I find this position highly unsatisfactory, and moreover not borne out by the evidence of the book of *Acts* itself. My great admiration and affection for my old teacher Martin Dibelius, whose lectures, seminars and personal friendship at Heidelberg before the war revealed not only the mind of a great scholar but also of a real man of God, must not prevent me from saying that, in my view, on this particular issue he has led New Testament scholarship off on a false scent.

No one would dispute the fact that taken as a whole the theology of the early chapters of *Acts* is less developed and less profound than the theology of Paul's letters. Scholars before Dibelius generally took this to mean that in these chapters we come very close to what the first Christians believed about God, about Christ, about the Church, about salvation. If we are to say now that the theology of *Acts* reflects the faith of the Church in the latter decades of the first century, we should have to label as an erratic not only St. Paul himself but also the authors of *Hebrews* and the Johannine literature, who are manifestly much more complex in their theology than the missionary preachers in the early chapters of *Acts*. J. C. O'Neill, the most radical of recent critics in his dating of *Acts*, which he places in the first half of the second century, is hard put to it to account for some of the titles given to Jesus in the book of *Acts*, titles which are not found or very rarely found elsewhere in the New Testament. The older view would have been that this is a clear indication of a stratum of

primitive theology which Luke has preserved. O'Neill
has to account for this awkward piece of evidence by
saying that 'chapters three, four and five [of *Acts*]
provide an exuberance of uncommon titles because
Luke is striving to give an archaic and scriptural ring to
that part of *Acts*.'[3]

If it is admitted that there is an archaic flavour about
the theology of *Acts* it is surely at least as likely that
this points in the direction of an author who knew that
this was the type of belief that was held in the earliest
years of the Church's existence, as that a literary artist
of a later date deliberately set out to embellish his
narrative with details which would evoke a picture of a
stage of history about which he knew relatively next
to nothing. C. H. Dodd in his seminal study of *The
Apostolic Preaching and its Developments*[4] contended
that the distinctively Hebraic character of the earlier
speeches in *Acts* indicated that the author had at his
disposal Aramaic sources of one kind or another, which
would of course take us back very close indeed to the
actual preaching of the first missionaries. But more
recently this has been disputed by scholars who claim
that the semitisms in *Acts* are either merely imitations
of the Septuagint or echoes of liturgical formulae.[5]

This basic conflict of opinion on the trustworthiness
of the speeches in *Acts* makes it possible for us to find
within the same covers of an important recent volume
of *Studies in Luke–Acts*, on the one hand Eduard
Schweizer maintaining with Dibelius that the speeches

[3] *Op. cit.*, p. 145.   [4] (London, 1936), pp. 34 ff.
[5] R. H. Fuller, *op. cit.*, p. 110.

in *Acts* are Luke's own composition, so that Paul speaks exactly like Peter and Peter exactly like Paul, and C. F. D. Moule on the other hand, insisting that this uniformity is not established and that Peter sometimes speaks like the Peter of the first epistle of *Peter* while Paul on occasion speaks like the Paul whom we know from his own letters. Yet, despite his claim that Luke was responsible for the contents of all the speeches, Schweizer is forced to admit that where Christ is spoken of in the early chapters of *Acts* Luke is drawing on older traditional material.[6] It would seem then that in what R. H. Fuller calls the post-Dibelian era, even within the ranks of those scholars who would not consider that in the speeches of *Acts* we have access to the thought of the first apostles but only to that of Luke, there is a recognition that some elements in these speeches and sermons are older than the finished products.[7]

Vincent Taylor said about the kenotic theory that if we dismiss it at the door it comes back through the window. The same thing might apparently be said about the reliability of Luke's evidence as to the beliefs of the early Church. However much the author of *Acts* may have contributed to the shaping of sermons and speeches that he puts into the mouths of Peter, Paul and Stephen, he does appear to have preserved in them not only individual characteristics which differentiate the

[6] Keck and Martyn (eds.) (New York, 1966) (E.E., London, 1968), pp. 214, 173 ff., 212.

[7] For a full discussion of this question, see M. Wilcox, *The Semitisms of Acts* (Oxford, 1965).

speakers but also elements which on any but the most sceptical view would seem to take us back into the earliest stratum of the Church's faith, as it was proclaimed in the first decades of its history.

Now no one doubts the sincerity or honesty of those scholars who would deny that the book of *Acts* is a trustworthy guide to the beliefs of the first Christians, but there seems to be such a thing as a built-in bias towards conservatism or radicalism which makes it possible for two scholars to examine the same evidence and come to diametrically-opposed conclusions. We may take as an example of this within the field that we are considering Paul's speech on Mars' Hill in *Acts* 17. As you will remember, according to the narrative of *Acts* St. Paul was invited by the philosophers of Athens to present the case for Christianity to them, which he did apparently without making much impression.

Dibelius had again led the modern trend with his essay on 'Paul on the Areopagus' as far back as 1939, in which he roundly maintained that the theology of the speech was foreign to Paul and to the whole of the New Testament. It was written by Luke as an example of a sermon to Gentiles in his own day, its ideas are Hellenistic not Jewish and its motifs are Stoic in origin. Only its conclusion can be described as in any way Christian. This approach has been followed by Conzelmann and Haenchen in their commentaries and specifically by Philipp Vielhauer in an influential article 'On the "Paulinism" of Acts' which has now been made widely available in English through its inclusion in the *Studies in Luke–Acts* to which I recently referred, although it appeared originally in German in 1950.[8] Vielhauer compares Paul's speech in Athens with the passage in *Romans* I in which Paul also deals with man's natural knowledge of God and comes to the conclusion that the two are incompatible. The speaker on the Areopagus is, he says, as distant from the real Paul as he is close to the second-century apologists.

An entirely opposite view, however, is taken by Bertil Gärtner in a special study entitled *The Areopagus Speech and Natural Revelation* published in 1955. Gärtner is critical of the whole Dibelian attitude to the speeches in *Acts*, and considers that they give reliable evidence of the apostolic message as it was preached by Peter and Paul. He draws attention to the personal characteristics which distinguish the different speakers, and underlines the different types of audience that they are addressing. He examines Paul's speech to the philosophers of Athens in detail and finds that while some of the ideas are expressed in a form which has affinities with Stoic thought—doubtless as a point of contact with the audience—the whole substance of the speech is thoroughly in line with Pauline theology as revealed in his letters, and derives wholly from Old Testament and Jewish tradition. He finds closer parallels to the ideas expressed in the speech in the Pentateuch, the Psalms, the Wisdom literature, the Apocrypha and the New Testament itself than in the pagan philosophers.

In a vital matter of this kind where we are concerned with the trustworthiness of the evidence for the beliefs of the first Christians and where equally competent

[8] *Op. cit.*, pp. 33–50.

scholars reach opposite conclusions we are not entitled
to dismiss the matter light-heartedly on the basis of
'you pays your money and you takes your choice'. I
would myself take the view that unless a clear and indisputable case can be made out for dismissing traditional views in biblical scholarship—such as for
example in the question of the unity of *Isaiah* or the
Pauline authorship of *Hebrews*—the benefit of the
doubt should always be given to the tradition of the
Church.

I have already suggested that the new look at the
author of *Acts* as a theologian in his own right is not
incompatible with the old look at Luke as a careful historian. In the matter of the sermons and speeches in
Acts, from which we should hope to distil the essence of
the earliest proclamation of the gospel and the faith of
the first Christians, I believe that we can reach conclusions which are reasonable and profitable without sub-
scribing to the view that the words that the author of
Acts has put into the mouths of Peter, Paul and
Stephen are the product of his own imagination.

Not even the most dyed-in-the-wool traditionalist
would contend that the speeches and sermons in *Acts*
are verbatim recordings of what the apostles said. Even
in these days of short speeches and potted sermons we
cannot get away with anything quite so potted as the
addresses in *Acts*. That Paul at any rate could outdo the
Puritans in the length of his sermons is evidenced by at
least one famous evening service when he went on
preaching till midnight with dire consequences for one
drowsy young member of the congregation (20:7 ff.). It

is therefore not a matter of dispute that what Luke gives us in *Acts* are summaries of sermons and speeches, and that to do this he exercised the function of an editor rather than that of a reporter.

How far this editorial function extended is the 64,000-dollar question and, as we have seen, one answer that has been frequently given in recent years is that the editor produced the sermons and speeches out of his own head. We may safely go part of the way with Dibelius and his disciples in conceding that there are sufficient similarities in the addresses that Luke incorporates in *Acts* to indicate that the same hand has been at work in shaping them all. There are indeed characteristic nuances and phrases which mark out one speaker from another, and the particular circumstances in which the sermon or speech was delivered result in noticeable differences in style. But that a single mind is behind them all, the mind of a singularly-gifted theologically-slanted historian appears to be beyond question.

As a by-product of the recent interest in historiography and its importance for New Testament studies, much attention has been given to parallels between the methods of the author of the book of *Acts* and those of ancient historians in general. The works of Jewish historians, such as Josephus and the writer of the books of the Maccabees, as well as those of classical historians, such as Suetonius and Tacitus, have been drawn into the discussion of how historians in roughly the same period as Luke dealt with the speeches which they included in their narratives.

It has been noted that some ancient historians felt themselves free on occasion to enliven their books with speeches which they regarded as some sort of light relief, to display their own skill in oratory or rhetoric. These flights of fancy were, however, condemned as irresponsible by the more sober writers of their time, and the canons of Thucydides in particular were followed by the most reputable authors. In a famous passage in his *History of the Peloponnesian War* Thucydides had said this: 'As for the speeches which were made by different men either when they were about to begin the war or when they were already engaged therein, it has been difficult to recall the words actually spoken with strict accuracy, both for me about what I myself heard and for those who from various other sources have brought me reports. So the speeches are given in the language in which, as it seemed to me, the several speakers would express, on the subjects under consideration, the sentiments most befitting the occasion, though at the same time I have adhered as closely as possible to the general sense of what was actually said.'[9]

This implies that Thucydides formulated the speeches in his narrative in his own words and in his own style on the basis of what he had actually heard if he was present himself, or what had been reported to him from people who had been there. Only when this kind of information failed him did he resort to composing the kind of speech that he believed the particular speaker would have made, in the light of what he knew

[9] *Hist.* I, 22; quoted by C. S. C. Williams, *op. cit.*, p. 36.

about his character and point of view. We may take it
that Luke was no less than Thucydides a reputable historian, who was not only, as a Gentile, guided by the
canons of pagan historiography but also, as a Christian,
debtor as well to the Old Testament and Jewish background which he shared with the missionaries whose sermons and speeches he had to record. If, as we have
earlier maintained, our author was no second-century
apologist or late first-century littérateur, but the companion of St. Paul on his journeys, with first-hand knowledge of some of the events he describes and ready
access to information about the earlier days before he
joined the missionary enterprise, we may be confident
that the sermons and speeches in the first half of the
book of *Acts*, covering roughly the first two decades of
Church history, give us in the Thucydidean 'general
sense' a reliable guide to the faith of the Church from
its beginning in Jerusalem on the first Whitsunday.

It is difficult to imagine that a theologically-minded
historian, writing, say, in the eighties, who was so
meticulous about recording the political and legal niceties of the fifties when he was himself involved in Paul's
campaigns, should not have taken the trouble to find
out from his many contacts what precisely had happened in the Church's infancy in the thirties and forties
and above all the precise terms in which the new faith
had been proclaimed. It was not Luke's own period. The
Church had expanded, and as he knew it first it was
making its impact on the Gentile world. But he was
writing a history of the Church from its beginnings,
and it was his business to find out what had been said

and done in that early and, to him, unfamiliar Palestinian setting when the gospel had been preached by Jews to Jews, before it had to be restated in terms that were meaningful to pagan minds.

In the nature of the case we should expect to find the theology of the first missionaries even more unfamiliar to us than it was to Luke. The faith of the Church in the twentieth century can no more be expressed in the same words as were used by the first apostles than in the precise terminology of the medieval churchmen, the Reformers or the nineteenth-century Evangelicals. But in every age the substance of the faith must be true to its historical origins. If there is development there must also be continuity and at every point in our history we must be ready to check current theological trends against the beliefs on which the Church was founded and which give it its only reason for existence.

When we are told by some theologians today that we can know little or nothing about the life of Jesus because the early Church was not interested in biographical details, or when we are told by others to think of God as the 'ground of being', or by others again not to think of Him at all because science has made Him redundant, or when in response to our plea that we must have something to hold on to as we lie out upon the deep, in Kierkegaard's words, with 70,000 fathoms of water under us, we are offered for our comfort Jesus 'the Man for others', we may well ask whether these meagre crumbs would have been enough to feed the 'noble army' of the Church's saints and martyrs, its poets, painters and composers, or the men who built its cathedrals. Nor if we are to judge by the book of *Acts* would they have satisfied the 'glorious company of the apostles' who laid its foundations.

It would be tedious in a public lecture of this kind to go through the sermons and speeches of the book of *Acts* with a tooth-comb and itemise the teaching of the first missionaries in detail. Luke had obviously no intention, even if he had had the necessary information, of providing his readers with a systematic exposition of the faith of the early Church. But he does tell us enough to enable us to have a sufficiently clear picture of what the first Christians believed and of how their beliefs were translated into action.

First and foremost stands the conception of God, transcendent and supreme, Creator of all that is and Lord of history. It was assumed that belief in the living God who had chosen Israel to be His own peculiar people, charged with the mission of bringing the world to the knowledge of its true obedience, who had revealed Himself through patriarch, prophet and psalmist and through His redemptive acts in the past, was the indispensable foundation of all faith. Since the first Christian missionaries were Jews addressing Jews they had no more hesitation than the Old Testament writers or Jesus Himself in speaking of God in robustly anthropomorphic terms. They would have been perplexed if they had been told that a future generation would feel that science and space travel had made it impossible any longer to speak of God as 'up there' or 'out there'. When St. Paul was faced with an audience at Athens which to some extent shared our modern attitude he had no difficulty in expressing the early Church's idea of God in a basically biblical way and at the same time couching it in language which made sense to pagan philosophers. The problem of communicating the faith is not a twentieth-century discovery.

In trying to present a picture of the faith of the earliest Christians I have given priority to their belief in God not only because the validity of such a belief is being questioned in our own day as it is, for example, by the 'Death of God' school of thought in America, but because I am a little alarmed at the present tendency among more radical theologians to discount the idea of God and to concentrate on Jesus. It is of course beyond dispute that Christ is the central figure—indeed in a sense the only figure—in the New Testament. It is also beyond dispute that He is not the central figure in other great religions. I am not by any means arguing for some kind of synthetic world-religion, but I am arguing that in all religions belief in an absolute or ultimate reality is basic, and that the first Christians, primarily St. Paul, proclaimed their faith as a fulfilment or completion of what men had believed before them. The earliest Christians, being Jews, thought of this in terms of the Old Testament revelation, but if their horizon had been wider, as became evident among the Christian Fathers, they would doubtless have seen a *praeparatio evangelica* in the widest possible terms as beginning with man's need for and response to God, which is basic to all religions, culminating as they believed in God's disclosure of Himself in Jesus. Unless we are prepared to say that the Church was mistaken in including the Old

Testament as part of its sacred scriptures we must recognise that the starting point of our faith as it was for the first Christians is the 'God and Father of our Lord Jesus Christ'.

It was because they had so profound a sense of the reality of the transcendent God, whose massive plan for the salvation of mankind had been disclosed in the story of Israel and recorded in the Old Testament, that they saw in Christ, in what He had said and done, and in His continuing presence with them, the culmination of God's mighty acts, the focus of worship and the power of new life. It took the mind of a Paul to comprehend the breadth and the length, the height and the depth of the fullness of God in Christ (*Eph.* 3:18–19), but even in its earliest days the Church acknowledged Him as its Lord and Saviour.

Some of the words that were used to describe Jesus seem to have been abandoned when the Church went out into the wider world. We find in *Acts* such titles for Jesus as the Servant or Child of God, the Son of Man, the Christ or Messiah, the Righteous One, all characteristic of a generation which was steeped in Old Testament thought and saw in Jesus the fulfilment of the hopes and prayers of psalmists and prophets. Little is said in the sermons in *Acts* about the events in the ministry of Jesus, and equally little about His teaching, for the obvious reason that Luke had already dealt with this fully in his earlier work, the third gospel. It has often been claimed that in *Acts* we find an adoptionist Christology, that there is no sign of recognition of the pre-existence of Christ, and that the significance of the

Cross is not yet appreciated. It is, however, by no means certain that all this is so, and a case can be made out for saying that a full Christology was present in embryo from the beginning.

What is abundantly clear, as C. F. D. Moule has shown in the admirable essay to which I have already referred, is that while there is a clear continuity between the Jesus of Nazareth in Luke's gospel and the Christ of *Acts*, the Christology of *Acts* is consistently 'exalted' in type. Jesus in *Acts* is never 'a mere prophet or rabbi of the past'. The fact of the Resurrection had made that view impossible. 'Jesus is shown in *Acts* as raised from death, exalted to heaven, destined ultimately to return, and meanwhile represented in the Church's activities and expansion by the Holy Spirit, whose advent is the result of Christ's "withdrawal".' The Resurrection is, as Moule says, 'the Christological watershed dividing the Gospel from the *Acts*'.[10]

In the last two lectures we shall be looking at what the book of *Acts* has to say about the Church and about the Holy Spirit. What the first Christians believed about them, as indeed about everything else, sprang from their basic conviction that the Resurrection of Jesus had been the turning point of history. When the period of reflection on the startling event of Easter Day and the significance of what preceded it had been rounded off by the visitation of the Spirit at Pentecost, the message that the first missionaries proclaimed in Jerusalem and from there outwards into the wider world was Good News of the signal and unmistakable evidence of God's crowning

[10] *Op. cit.*, pp. 165–6.

mercy of which they themselves had first-hand knowledge. In the words and deeds of Jesus they had seen the love of God in action. This exhilarating sense of the possibility of new life in a sombre world had been dashed by the Crucifixion when it seemed as if the power of evil was stronger than the power of God. The Resurrection had changed all that as they had now come to understand, and the impulse to spread the Good News was, from Pentecost onwards, irresistible.

What Jesus had meant when He spoke of His own role as the fulfilment of Isaiah's picture of the Servant of God who would give His life for the sins of the world was now clear. The past had been blotted out in a mighty act of deliverance. St. Paul affirms that when he became a Christian one of the traditions he was taught, and therefore one of the themes of the earliest preaching, was 'that Christ died for our sins according to the Scriptures' (I *Cor*. 15: 3). As G. B. Caird says: 'Without the Resurrection there could have been no Christianity: yet the Resurrection was no isolated event. The first preachers did not proclaim to the world that a resurrection had occurred. They preached the Resurrection of the Crucified. Nowhere in the New Testament is there any justification for separating these twin pillars of the Gospel. The Resurrection vindicated the innocence of Jesus and revealed His death as a mystery of divine love, while the Crucifixion gave to men the assurance that the Risen One was also the Saviour.'[11]

At such a time of theological uncertainty and confusion as we are at present passing through it is salutary

[11] *The Apostolic Age* (London, 1955), p. 43.

to remind ourselves that the faith on which the Church was founded was neither a demythologised version of the historical legacy of the Old Testament, nor an anaemic accommodation to the secularism of the pagan world, but a full-blooded proclamation of the transcendence of God, the Lordship of Christ and the forgiveness of sins. Together with these, as we shall see later, went unequivocal claims as to the unique role of the Church and the supernatural powers of the Holy Spirit. Indeed, it would seem that even if we say that the earliest credal affirmation was something as simple as 'Jesus is Lord', the later formulation of the Faith at greater length is not unjustly called the Apostles' Creed, because the evidence of the book of *Acts* is that in essence this was the Faith which the apostles proclaimed. Whatever restatement of what is claimed to be outmoded terminology may be thought necessary to make the Faith of the Church intelligible to modern man, the sermons and speeches in the first half of the book of *Acts* leave us in no doubt as to the basic beliefs on which the Church was founded. To modify or whittle these beliefs away in a misguided attempt to reconcile Christianity with current trends of thought is to emasculate the Faith and rob the gospel of its God-given power to cure the world of its sickness and to bring meaning, purpose and hope into the lives of ordinary men and women.

V. THE FORM OF THE CHURCH

THOMAS J. J. ALTIZER, of Emory University, Texas, is generally reckoned to be the foremost exponent of the new and radical 'Death of God' theology which has erupted in the United States. Among other things he says 'there is no reason why Christianity should be identified with its ecclesiastical expressions' and he traces back much of our present trouble to the 'false identification of Christianity with the Christian Church'. He calls for 'theologians with the courage and faith to recognise and celebrate the fact that we are living in a post-Christian age' and claims that 'no longer is theology tied to the Church, for the first duty of the Christian theologian must be seen as, not loyalty to the Church, but loyalty to Christ, that is, loyalty to Christ as he is met in the totality of human experience'.[1] To quote Altizer's own words in his most recent book, *The Gospel of Christian Atheism*: 'From the point of view of radical Christianity, the original heresy was the identification of the Church as the body of Christ.'[2]

We are, of course, not concerned in these lectures with a critique of the present radical trend in American

[1] J. C. Cooper, *The Roots of the Radical Theology* (Philadelphia, 1967) (E.E., London, 1968), p. 118.

[2] (London, 1967), p. 132.

theology as represented by Altizer, Hamilton and van Buren, but Altizer's view of the relationship between Christ and the Church which I have just referred to is directly relevant to our subject. For if he is right in saying that in the twentieth century our first loyalty must be to Christ and not to the Church, this would appear to be difficult to reconcile with the attitude of the first Christians, who would not have understood that such a dichotomy was possible. Whatever discrepancies occur in Luke's three accounts of the conversion of St. Paul, the words which the apostle claims to have heard never vary: 'Saul, Saul, why do you persecute me?' (9:4; 22:7; 26:14). Paul had had no hand in the trial and death of Jesus but he had, we are told, 'made havoc of the Church' (8:3) and on the Damascus road he was confronted with the truth that Christ and His Church are inseparable.

We may not be able to go all the way with J. A. T. Robinson in his excellent little book *The Body*, when he asserts that 'the appearance on which Paul's whole faith and apostleship was founded was the revelation of the resurrected body of Christ, not as an individual, but as the Christian community'.[3] Some of us would perhaps find it difficult to grasp imaginatively how St. Paul could have had an encounter with the Risen Christ of such a kind as to make him identify Him at once with the Church. But quite clearly, both in his own letters and in Luke's accounts of his conversion in *Acts*, there was in Paul's mind a relationship between Christ and the Church which would have made it impossible for

[3] (London, 1952), p. 58.

him to accept Altizer's proposition.

However, it is not only in the mind of St. Paul that Christ and His Church are conceived to be inextricably bound together. The terms in which the first Christians expressed this, according to Luke's account in *Acts*, are no longer current coinage but the convictions that lay behind them are beyond question. Jesus was the Messiah for whom Israel had long waited. By putting Him to death, as they had done with the prophets who spoke of His coming, said Stephen at his trial before the Sanhedrin (ch. 7), the Jews had finally forfeited their claim to be the People of God. By the same token, in accepting Jesus as both Messiah and Lord His followers fulfilled the role of the Remnant of which Isaiah had spoken. They were the new Israel.

In this conception of the nature of their community the first Christians were faithful to the intention of Jesus. It is clear both from His choice of twelve disciples, symbolic of the twelve tribes of Israel, and from His institution of a new covenant to replace the covenant of Sinai, that Jesus' purpose was to create a new People of God which would be at once continuous with old Israel yet freed from its restrictive practices, and which would take over Israel's historic assignment to bring the world to the knowledge of God. So in its earliest days the young community, in obedience to the intention of its Founder, filled the twelfth place in the apostolate which had been made vacant by Judas, so that the symbolic structure of the new Israel should be preserved.

When St. Paul speaks of the Church as the Body of

Christ, or when he equates being in the Church with being in Christ, he is not importing into Christianity ideas which are foreign to its character or novel in its development. By the very nature of their Old Testament background and Hebrew upbringing the first Christians could not think of the Messiah apart from Israel, or of themselves as the Remnant being in any way separable from either. When Stephen at his trial has a vision of Jesus as Son of Man, he sees Him in the role which Jesus claimed for Himself in His own trial before Caiaphas (*Mark* 14:62). Both go back to *Daniel* 7:13, where the mysterious figure of the Son of Man is at once Head of the new community of the kingdom of the saints and representative of it. The witness of the book of *Acts* to the earliest stratum of Christian belief is thus that Christ and His people are one, Jesus and His Church are inseparably united. If we accept Altizer's suggestion that we should concentrate our attention on Christ and more or less dismiss the organised Church as irrelevant, we must recognise that in so doing we are creating something which whatever we call it cannot be called Christianity.

But what was the form of the Church in its earliest stage as we see it in the book of *Acts*? John Allegro, whatever he thinks of its present manifestations, has no doubt that the organisation of the early Church was largely dependent on the Essene pattern. In a veritable spate of newspaper articles on the occasion of the recent exhibition in this country of some of the Dead Sea Scrolls, Allegro dismissed the gospels as the product of Christian myth-makers, who modelled their picture of

Jesus on the Teacher of Righteousness of the Qumran sect, and who built the Church on the lines of the Righteous Teacher's community. He claimed that not only is the office of the Christian bishop founded on the office of the 'inspector' or 'overseer' (*mebaqqer*) of the Essene community, but the source of the names and offices of the original apostles is to be sought in the administrative structure of the Qumran sect.

Amid the welter of publications on the Dead Sea Scrolls, and despite Allegro's charge that Christian scholars are too prejudiced to face up to the implications for the Church and for New Testament theology of the Qumran discoveries, we have come a long way from the first orthodox reactions to the exaggerated claims of Dupont Sommer[4] and Edmund Wilson.[5] It would be agreed by most scholars today that there are parallels between the practices of the Dead Sea sect and the early Church. Both were protestant movements which sought to reform Jewish religion. Both were lay communities dedicated to the pursuit of truth and holiness. Both could be called followers of a Righteous Teacher and both were awaiting the Messianic Age. They believed in the sharing of their possessions, they partook of a sacred ritual meal and they practised baptism. Both of them called themselves 'the elect' and followers of 'the Way'.

None of this need surprise us when we remember their common period, locality and background, their common Old Testament heritage, and their noncon-

---

[4] *The Dead Sea Scrolls* (Oxford, 1952).
[5] *The Scrolls from the Dead Sea* (New York, 1955).

formist origins. It would be more surprising if the organisation of the early Church owed nothing to an older, well-established and to all accounts efficiently-administered neighbouring sectarian movement. But this is something quite different from saying that the Christian Church was the creation of dispossessed Essenes, who imposed on it the pattern of their own community life, and reinterpreted their own beliefs into Christian myths in order to propagate their teaching more successfully in the Gentile world.

It may be, as has been suggested by several scholars, that after the destruction of the monastery at Qumran in A.D. 68, large numbers of the Dead Sea sect joined the young Christian Church and brought with them their more rigid tradition of discipline and order. It is also possible that among the 'great number of priests' referred to in *Acts* 6:7 who were converted to Christianity, some at any rate were Essenes and that through them Essene influences penetrated into the life of the Church.

It does not seem, however, as if these influences, such as they were, made any marked impression on the life of the Church in the earliest stage of all with which we are concerned. Father Joseph Fitzmyer has made a careful study of *Jewish Christianity in Acts in the light of the Qumran Scrolls*,[6] in which he examines the parallels between Essene and early Christian practice in such matters as terminology, sharing of property, the use of the Old Testament, organisational structure and the common meal. He concludes that these features of

[6] Keck and Martyn, *op. cit.*, pp. 233–57.

Essene tenets and practices 'often shed important light on passages of *Acts* that describe the early Jewish Christian Church'. He considers that 'it is possible at times to think in terms of a direct contact or a direct imitation of Essene usage' (as in the common designation of both Christianity and the Qumran community as 'the Way'), but he rightly insists that we 'cannot prove from such points of contact that the early Jewish Christian Church developed out of an exclusively Essene framework', and that the most that we can say is that the early Church was 'not without some influence from the Essenes'. In his view 'the influence of Qumran literature on *Acts* is not as marked as it is in other New Testament writings, for example *John, Paul, Matthew* and *Hebrews*', and that such parallels as do exist, 'striking though they may be, are not numerous'.

We have long been familiar with the fanciful claim that Jesus Himself was an Essene, and the less fanciful possibility that John the Baptist may have had some relationship with the Qumran community. It would be foolish to deny that both Jesus and John the Baptist, or for that matter St. Paul, may have had some contact with the sect, and that evidence of this may be detected in their teaching and practice. Similarly with the early Church. It has never been the claim of Christianity that its authority rests on its complete originality. Apart from anything else, its obvious dependence on the faith and morals of the Old Testament would preclude any such suggestion. If the Dead Sea Scrolls now indicate that it was indebted also to nonconformist as well as to mainstream Judaism, we may echo G. R. Driver's verdict that in the last analysis it is 'the person and position of Christ which makes the ultimate difference between the Gospel and the Scrolls'[7] and, by the same token, between the Church and the Qumran community.

Before passing from the Dead Sea Scrolls and the question of how they can help us to understand various aspects of early Church practice, it may be useful to draw attention to an article by Bo Reicke of Basel in Krister Stendahl's important symposium *The Scrolls and the New Testament*.[8] Reicke begins his essay which he calls 'The Constitution of the Primitive Church in the light of Jewish Documents' by noting that it is not only the apologists for the three major ecclesiastical systems—episcopalian, presbyterian and congregationalist—who find justification for their particular form of Church government in the constitution of the primitive Church but also that allegedly dispassionate New Testament scholars and Church historians can, after examination of the New Testament evidence, reach radically different conclusions as to what exactly was the pattern of Church order in the earliest stage of the Church's history. Even allowing for the fact that not even theologians and Church historians can rid themselves of subjective preconceptions in approaching the material, depending on their own particular tradition, it is obvious that the problem is extremely complex. Reicke argues that the reason for this is that the organisation of the early Church was itself highly complex, and not

[7] Quoted: M. Black, *N.T.S.*, Vol. 13, No. 1, p. 89.
[8] (London, 1958), pp. 143–56.

in accordance with the order of any one of the three main claimants to New Testament authority for their own system of government.

There is no doubt that even without resorting to the Pastoral epistles, where the position of Timothy and Titus might point in the direction of monarchic or episcopal administration, the book of *Acts* indicates that Peter, and later James, occupied the role of head of the first Christian community in Jerusalem. We could, if we like, call James a bishop. Yet side by side with this is the fact that the oligarchic or presbyterian system was represented by the Twelve Apostles, and later by the appointment of the Seven and of a special class of elders. Nevertheless, despite the distinctive role that apostles and presbyters had to play, the congregation as a whole had its own distinctive function. On two occasions—the election of the twelfth apostle in *Acts* 1 and the Council of Jerusalem in *Acts* 15—the congregation seems to have played more than a passive role. The specific number of the one hundred and twenty, who are said to have been present at the election of Matthias to the vacancy in the apostolate, was in Jewish constitutional law the required number for the election of members of the Sanhedrin. This suggests that only by the presence of the congregation could the election of Matthias by the apostles be regarded as legally correct. Similarly the decree of the Council of Jerusalem was promulgated as the decision of 'the apostles and the elders with the whole church' (15:22).

Thus it would seem that in the Jerusalem Church, the mother congregation of Christianity, tendencies towards the three mainstream traditions—episcopal, presbyterian and congregationalist—existed side by side without being mutually exclusive or without coming into conflict. Reicke describes this pattern of the primitive Church as 'nonegalitarian, hierarchic and yet organically unified' and goes on from there to examine the constitution of the Qumran community and that of the Covenanters of Damascus, as evidenced in their respective texts, the Manual of Discipline and the Damascus Document, which show that they both belonged to the same religious movement and to a milieu which was chronologically and geographically very close to early Christianity.

Reicke's study suggests that, while it would be quite wrong to maintain, as Allegro has done for example, that the early Church based its constitution on the Essene pattern, there are sufficiently striking analogies between them to enable us to understand better how it came about that the ministry of the early Church gradually developed in a monarchical direction as a result of its oriental background. As shedding light upon the earliest period, however, with which we are concerned, Reicke's conclusion after examination of the Qumran and Damascus texts is worth recording, that in the constitution of both these Essene communities, the *mebaqqer*, that is the 'superintendent' or 'moderator', the leading men, and the community as a whole had all a part to play.

'The two Jewish documents,' he says, 'which are close to primitive Christianity in terms of both geography and time, indicate a constitutional structure which is, in a very specific sense, "complex". Monarchic, oligarchic, and democratic tendencies exist side by side without open contention. In spite of the drastically unequal importance of the members, the community forms an organic unity. This was clearly the case,' he goes on, 'in the primitive church as well, although the hierarchic stratification of the various members is much more strongly expressed in the Jewish documents. He who wants to appeal to the New Testament in matters of contemporary church order may take notice of the fact that in a Jewish movement slightly older than Christianity or contemporary with it, monarchic, oligarchic and democratic tendencies could work together in organic unity. And yet its members were not nearly so closely united as the brothers in Christ were soon to feel themselves.'

Among recent German writers on Luke, it has been maintained, particularly by Ernst Käsemann, that our author's ecclesiastical background is 'primitive Catholicism' (*Frühkatholizismus*). Vielhauer, for example, says that Luke 'no longer stands within earliest Christianity, but in the nascent early catholic Church' and Käsemann himself asserts that 'the Lucan writings as a whole cannot be understood until we realise that for Luke it is only within the stream of apostolic tradition that one belongs to the *Una Sancta* as the earthly place of salvation'.[9]

Catholicism, primitive or present day, is a loaded word for some Protestants. It is difficult, however, to see why it should be regarded as a criticism of Luke if he

[9] Keck and Martyn, *op. cit.*, pp. 49, 63.

shows that the primitive Church was catholic in the sense that we mean when we affirm in the creed that we believe in 'one holy catholic and apostolic Church'. C. K. Barrett is alarmed when Käsemann says that in *Acts* 'the Word is no longer the single criterion of the Church, but the Church legitimises the Word, and the apostolic origin of ecclesiastical office affords the guarantee for legitimate preaching'. Barrett thinks that when we use the phrase 'primitive Catholicism' we ought to mean the attitude to the Church reflected in the letters of Clement and Ignatius[10] with their 'ecclesiastical, ministerial, authoritarian and sacramental' emphasis. By contrast Luke, according to Barrett, sees the apostles not as administrators but as preachers of the Word, and the Church not as 'a hierarchical *Heilsanstalt* [or agency of salvation] but as a loosely-knit evangelistic and pastoral organism'.[11]

R. R. Williams, commenting on this says: 'Dr. Barrett, when he reads *Acts*, sees in it a classical picture of the early Church already well-committed to the Reformed doctrine of the Word of God,' and continues, 'I trust I shall be forgiven if, as an Anglican Bishop, I see in it a Church equally governed by, and devoted to, the Word of God, but also a Church in which the institutional arrangements—ministry, sacraments, and calendar—have their part to play in the preservation and propagation of that Word.' Most of us would probably agree with Williams.

Mainstream Christianity, to use the B.B.C. terminology, has always relied on *Acts*, as Williams points out,

[10] c. A.D. 95 and 115.   [11] *Op. cit.*, pp. 70 ff.

for justification of many of its practices. The com-
memoration of Ascension Day and of Whitsunday goes
back to *Acts* 1 and 2. The celebration of Holy Com-
munion on the first day of the week is taken to be
exemplified in the service at Troas in *Acts* 20 when Paul
preached his record-breaking sermon. We learn from
Acts that baptism was the normal rite of admission to
the Church, and some would find justification for infant
baptism in the administration of this sacrament to the
Philippian jailer and 'all his family' (16:33). The laying
on of hands by the apostles in the case of those recently
baptised has been regarded as the original pattern for
confirmation, and so on.[12] The early Church was obviously more than just a collection of preaching centres.

It confuses the issue, however, to say that we find
evidence in *Acts* for any particular form of the Church
as we know it today. The earliest Christians were not
Anglican or Reformed, or even primitive Catholics in
the Ignatian sense. No branch of the Church can claim
to reproduce in its present practice or structure the
Church that Luke describes in *Acts*. All branches—including Pentecostalists, Salvation Army and Quakers—
may claim to be in continuity with it in that they
worship the same Lord and live by the same Spirit. But
is this enough? Some branches of the Church would say
No, and would claim proprietary rights to be the only
true Church or to have certain features which are
essential to the Church. May we turn then to look at the
evidence of *Acts* itself?

[12] *Historicity and Chronology in the New Testament*, D. E.
Nineham (ed.) (London, 1965), pp. 145, 160.

Before we do that, however, I must come back for a moment to the question of the reliability of Luke's information. If we are dealing with a late first-century or early second-century theologian, who either reflects the concerns of the Church of his own times, or creates an artificial picture of a period of Church history about which he knew next to nothing, then it does not really matter very much to us today what he has to say about the form of the Church in its earliest days. Like the faith of the Church in the same period it would be Luke's own brain-child, of some interest, certainly, but not vital to the current ecumenical discussion.

If on the other hand, as I have tried to establish, there is every reason to believe that our author was himself involved in part of the story which he describes in *Acts*, and for the earlier part of his book had easy access to accurate information about what went on before he joined Paul's missionary enterprise, then we must take what he says about the earliest form of the Church very seriously indeed. Since his book as a whole reveals him, as we have seen, to be a man who took the trouble to record the niceties of the provincial and legal administration of the Empire in his day, and to be a stickler for accuracy in geographical details, it would surely be reasonable to expect that he would be no less concerned to get his facts right on ecclesiastical policy in the first three decades of Church history which form the subject of his narrative.

Should it be, therefore, that what emerges from Luke's pages is a Church whose form is in many respects imprecise and often obscure, it would be wrong to conclude that Luke did not know any better. On the contrary, it would be more likely that he knew only too well that in the period he is describing the Church was finding its feet, and that consequently it has no absolute form or order which in some way constitutes its essence and from which it must never depart if it is still to be called the Church. What in fact we find is that certain features are present in a primary form which later become more significant, and that certain other features which seem to have been regarded as even more important are for one reason or another gradually dropped. In other words it is very much easier to glean from the book of *Acts* what is of the essence of the Church in matters of faith, than it is to say what is of its essence in matters of Church order. As we have seen, there are certain postulates of belief which from the beginning have been regarded as integral to Christianity, which, we might almost say, cannot be discarded if we are to maintain that we still hold to the Christian Faith in any recognisable sense. The same cannot be said for the form of the Church as it is described in the book of *Acts*.

Let us begin with the Church itself, the *ecclesia*. We have seen already that the first believers, being Jews, regarded themselves as the new Israel committed to the service of the Messiah whom God had sent, and whom they now acknowledged as their risen Lord. They came to call themselves the Church, using the word *ecclesia*, because it linked them with their Old Testament background as the new People of God. But on the evidence of *Acts* their earliest description of themselves was 'the brethren', or 'the disciples', or 'all who believed'. The word 'church' in *Acts* usually means the local congregation, and looked at together the young congregations are spoken of as the 'churches'. Only twice is the word 'Church' used to mean the whole company of Christians, and there is no suggestion that St. Paul's later conception of the Church as the Body of Christ, or St. John's doctrine of the mystical union of Christ with His Church, had as yet been envisaged. Indeed Luke on occasions uses the word *ecclesia* to denote a pagan assembly.

There is a similar lack of precision in the sacramental life of the Church. Baptism was insisted on as a rite of admission, but it seems to have been much more akin to John the Baptist's baptism of repentance for the forgiveness of sins, than to the Pauline or Johannine conception of baptismal regeneration. Again St. Paul and St. John emphasise the deep significance of the Eucharist. Luke knew all about this too, for he had recorded its institution at the Last Supper in his gospel. But although it looks as if regular eucharistic celebrations were an integral part of the life of the earliest Christians (2:42), they seem to have formed part of a communal meal and are described simply as the 'breaking of bread' (2:46). Similarly the laying on of hands by the apostles, which has been thought in the case of the Seven to have been an act of ordination (6:6), was administered to all and sundry in the case of the Samaritan converts (8:17).

When we turn to the government of the Church in its earliest days, the situation is equally fluid and imprecise.

To begin with, the Twelve Apostles dominate the scene, but more as the embodiment of the new Israel, as former companions of Jesus, and as witnesses to His Resurrection, than as a supreme ecclesiastical court. St. Peter, who receives most mention, appears primarily in the role of an active evangelist. The others, generally unspecified, were presumably also travelling missionaries. The teaching of the Apostles, which for Luke means their preaching, was regarded as the authoritative proclamation of the gospel, and the Twelve are shown as being principally concerned that new missionary ventures, as for example those among the Samaritans and the Gentiles, should be inspected and approved as being in line with Jewish-Christian practice.

After the Council of Jerusalem they disappear from Luke's record, and no mention is made of any successors being appointed to preserve continuity of their office. The Twelve occupy a unique place, but there are others whom Luke also calls apostles, Paul and Barnabas, for example (14:14), and even more anonymous evangelists who established Christian communities in Phoenicia, Cyprus, Damascus and Antioch, when they had been driven out of Jerusalem after Stephen's martyrdom. Stephen had been one of the Seven appointed by the Jerusalem mother-church, ostensibly to assist the Twelve, though they are called neither 'deacons' nor 'elders'. More likely they were appointed to placate the more radically-minded Greek-speaking section of the Christian community.

We find James, the Lord's brother, emerging as head of the local Jerusalem church, presumably on account of his relationship to Jesus, and associated with him are presbyters or elders. When the Church expands into the Gentile world it seems to have been the practice of St. Paul to appoint elders to look after the young congregations after the initial missionary campaign (14:23). At one point these elders are called *episkopoi*, or bishops (20:28), so that at this stage the two offices are the same. On the other hand the local church at Antioch seems to have been led by men who are described as 'prophets' and 'teachers' (13:1).

Thus the overall picture of the government of the Church as a whole in its earliest stage is one of diversity, which we might even call pragmatic. Apart from the unique position of the Twelve Apostles there is no common pattern, and certainly nothing that could be called Church 'order' in the modern sense. Leadership was essential in each congregation, but it seems to have been stereotyped neither in form nor designation. As we know, by the second century the three-fold ministry of bishops, priests and deacons was the accepted pattern, and by the fourth century the bishop of Rome had established his claim to the papacy. It is no argument against either the three-fold ministry or the papacy to say that neither was in existence in the first stage of the Church's history. Both may very well maintain that they have developed naturally from it in response to the demands of an expanding Church, and for a variety of reasons a combination of both, with obviously necessary modifications, may come to be universally recognised as the most effective pattern of administration for the whole Church as it seeks to fulfil its appointed mission in the world. What no branch of the Church today can claim, however, Roman, Orthodox, Anglican or Reformed, is that its own particular form of Church order entitles it to call itself the true Church as it has been from the beginning, to the exclusion of the rest or some of the rest.

In the earliest stage of the Church there was no more a parity of ministry or a three-fold ministry, than there was a patriarchate or a papacy. All these present forms of Church government can be described as legitimate developments occasioned by historical events and the demands of particular situations. There is nothing absolute or essential in any of them, if we are to be guided by the original practice of the first Christians. The authority and continuity of the Church was safeguarded, not by apostolic succession but by adherence to the apostolic tradition concerning Jesus, by the legacy of the Old Testament and by the presence of the Spirit. In the light of the evidence of the book of *Acts*, any Christian community which reflects these characteristics, whether it be of Salvationists, Quakers, Pentecostalists or Brethren, is as much a part of the true Body of Christ in the New Testament sense as are those branches of the Church which have more rigid systems of government.

When we talk of 'our unhappy divisions' the phrase is only superficially true. All Christians are in the deepest sense united, for there is only one Church, one Body of Christ of which all Christians are members. No one was more convinced of this than St. Paul, and perhaps we may leave the last word on this subject to him. In his

letter to the young Galatian churches, whose foundation Luke so vividly describes in *Acts*, he is arguing
against circumcision as being the true criterion of
membership of the Church, which would inevitably
have led to a division between Jewish-Christians and
Gentile-Christians. He might have argued that the
Church must be seen to be one in order to present a
united front against a pagan world, or that unity is de-
sirable for practical reasons, such as economy of re-
sources or greater efficiency.

Instead, he takes his stand on the principle that
membership of the Body of Christ depends on acceptance of Jesus as Son of God, Saviour and Lord, and that
ancient and hallowed traditions, such as circumcision,
are quite irrelevant. He assumed that incorporation into
the Church by baptism, which was not a matter of
dispute, was the outward sign of inward commitment,
but we may well wonder whether, if he had been pressed,
he would not in the last resort have equated baptism
with circumcision as a significant rite but not essential
to salvation. In the present ecumenical situation it
would seem that St. Paul would urge us to accept each
other as we are, with full and formal recognition of the
validity of each other's traditions, as being the first step
towards organic unity, rather than to insist on certain
criteria of ministry and sacraments, which in Paul's
view cannot be regarded as anything more than acci-
dents of history. We have so much to learn from each
other, and I say this as a member of the Church of
Scotland who, as an adherent of the Church of England
for the past fifteen years, with some acquired knowledge

of English nonconformity, has seen at first hand much of the strength and weakness of presbyterianism, episcopacy and Free Church systems of government. But we cannot fully learn from each other unless we first pull down the man-made barriers, in order to live and work and, above all, grow together.

VI. THE GOSPEL OF THE HOLY SPIRIT

ONE of the prescribed topics of these Croall lectures according to the disposition of their founder is 'The Person and Work of the Holy Spirit'. So far as I have been able to discover, the Holy Spirit has only once since the foundation of the lectures in 1872 formed the subject of a whole series. This was about forty years ago when Professor H. M. B. Reid took as his theme: 'The Holy Spirit and the Mystics'. It is perhaps not without significance that the Holy Spirit was linked with mysticism in this way by Professor Reid, since most people would probably agree that next to the doctrine of the Trinity the doctrine of the Holy Spirit is the most mysterious and elusive concept for teachers or preachers of the Christian faith to define or explain.

According to the Nicene Creed the Holy Spirit is 'the Lord, the giver of life' and, as Oliver Quick points out,[1] the difficulty of formulating a precise doctrine of the Holy Spirit is partly that 'the nature of all life, and therefore of its giver, can only be learned gradually by living', and partly that it is the Holy Spirit Himself who is 'the source of vital knowing and the light in which objects are truly known'. Yet if, as Quick says, 'in its widest range the doctrine of the Holy Spirit is nothing

[1] O. C. Quick, *Doctrines of the Creed* (London, 1938), p. 271.

else than the doctrine of the manner and method of the presence and activity of the living God in his created world', this is exactly what the book of *Acts* is about, and this is why it has been so often called 'The Gospel of the Holy Spirit'.

Luke, although he has clearly a theological turn of mind, is not a professional theologian of the calibre of St. Paul, and we should not expect from him a doctrinal exposition of his convictions on the subject of the Spirit in the Pauline manner. What we should expect, and what we get, is a practical demonstration of the Spirit at work. For Luke, everything that happens in the life of the Church from the beginning to the end of his story is in one way or another controlled, inspired and furthered by the Holy Spirit. He sees the Church as the People of God advancing towards the fulfilment of God's purpose for the world, not in their own strength but in the power of the Spirit. It is a Spirit-filled Church, and its members are ordinary men and women who have been endowed with this unique gift from God.

As in the case of their attitude to Christ, where they were more concerned with His past and present activity than with formulating any doctrine about His relationship to God, so in the case of the Holy Spirit the first Christians did not attempt to systematise their views. Because they were Jews they could on occasion speak of the Holy Spirit almost as a personification of God (e.g. 15:28), like Wisdom in the minds of the Wisdom Scribes, but mostly, and certainly in the beginning, the Spirit was more simply regarded as the power of God at work in human affairs. As W. L. Knox has put it: 'It would seem that *Acts* reflects the gradual and quite unrationalised development by which the relation of the Spirit to God in Himself and to Jesus as the exalted Christ is passing from its purely Jewish form of belief in a spiritual action of God or the Lord on the mind and soul of the disciple into the later Christian conception of a "person" within the divine Trinity. His relation to God and to Christ seems to be completely vague and undetermined.'[2]

Similarly there is no clear cut theological or ecclesiastical pattern of how and when the Spirit can be expected to be given. Normally it is thought of as accompanying baptism on admission into the new community. St. Peter said to the crowd at Pentecost: 'Repent and be baptised . . . and you will receive the gift of the Holy Spirit' (2:38). But the Samaritan converts to Christianity were baptised, we are told, without receiving the Spirit, which only happened to them later through the laying on of hands by the apostles (8:12–17). Yet it was obviously not invariably channelled through the apostles or through the laying on of hands by anyone at all. Cornelius and his family circle, we are told, received the gift of the Spirit before they were baptised (10:44–48), and the apostles themselves received the Spirit at Pentecost while, as far as we know, they may never have been baptised at all.

Yet however imprecise the first Christians may have been in this as in other respects—so imprecise as to refer to the Holy Spirit in Peter's words as 'this thing'

[2] *Op. cit.*, p. 92.

(2 : 33)—they were never in any doubt as to its reality as a new power which had come into their experience at Pentecost. Schooled as they were on Old Testament prophecy, they had been taught by Isaiah, Ezekiel, Joel and Zechariah to associate a great outpouring of the Spirit of God with the coming of the Messiah and the birth of a new age. Jesus Himself had pointed to His own ministry as proof that the Spirit was mightily at work (*Luke* 11 : 20), and His Resurrection had convinced His followers that they were now living in the time of which the prophets had spoken.

Their minds were thus prepared, in Luke's interpretation of the situation, by the absence of the Spirit after Christ's Ascension to expect its return, as happened at Pentecost. The Holy Spirit of God which had been seen at work uniquely in the words and works of Jesus was now being given by Christ to His Church to continue His work in the world. It is not surprising, in view of the remarkable events which the apostles had themselves seen in the ministry and Resurrection of Jesus, that it was the more dramatic evidence of the presence of the Spirit, such as speaking with tongues, miracles and prophecy, that at first attracted most attention. It would be a complete travesty of the situation, however, to think that these were ever regarded as mere marvels or portents, or to overlook the fact that side by side with them from the beginning went the recognition of the presence of the Spirit in less spectacular ways as the power that could change men's lives and build a Christian community.

Whether the tradition of the absence of the Spirit

between the Ascension and Pentecost came to Luke, as Knox suggests,[3] as a symbolic parallel with the rabbinical story that Moses was summoned to heaven to receive the Torah, which he then brought down to men, in which case Christ was regarded as sending down the new Law at Pentecost to be written on men's hearts, or whether, as Conzelmann maintains,[4] the idea comes from Luke himself, to make a clear distinction between the period of Christ and the period of the Church and the Spirit in the divine economy, the day of Pentecost marks the beginning of the Church's mission.

Like the story of the Ascension, the story of Pentecost is to be read as a pictorial expression of a theological fact rather than as a literal description of a particular event. What hand Luke himself had in the shaping of it is impossible to say. The symbols of wind and fire, suggesting the divine presence, express the profound spiritual experience which the apostles shared on the first Whitsunday. We may hazard the guess that the overpowering religious ecstasy, which issued in 'speaking with tongues' or glossolalia, was communicated to the more sympathetic in the crowd, giving rise to the tradition of a 'miracle of languages', while the less sympathetic regarded the apostles as being merely under the influence of drink.

The Old Testament prophets had to some extent been similarly caught up in such ecstatic experiences and Peter had no doubt that this was the great outpouring of the Spirit of which Joel had spoken. It was the first, but by no means the last, occasion in the story of the

[3] *Op. cit.*, p. 85 f.   [4] *The Theology of St. Luke*, p. 184.

early Church as recorded in *Acts* and in St. Paul's letters where this undoubtedly genuine religious experience came upon individuals and groups. Paul's concern in his letter to the church at Corinth, where he seeks to keep this particular manifestation of the presence of the Spirit within the bounds of decorum during divine service, is no criticism of the reality of the experience. It has recurred at many points in the history of the Church and it is a feature of early Christianity which is preserved among Pentecostalists today. With regard to its present practice, if we are to be guided by St. Paul, we may echo J. P. M. Sweet's judicious conclusion in a recent article on the subject,[5] that 'we must reject any claim that tongues are the exclusive or even the normal sign that a Christian has received the Spirit' and that 'his [Paul's] authority cannot be claimed for regarding glossolalia as a necessary part of Christian life'. The most we can say—but with the authority and emphasis of Jesus Himself—is: do not forbid it (I *Cor.* 14:37–39) and, on Paul's own authority: do not quench the Spirit (I *Thess.* 5:19).

I remember when I was a student talking to my old headmaster about the kind of scripture teaching we had been regaled with at school. My recollection is that in Glasgow Academy over forty years ago now it never seemed to get much beyond the more lurid episodes in the book of *Judges*. I suggested therefore that we might have been better employed studying the book of *Acts*. The headmaster's reply was: 'Far too difficult for boys—nothing but miracles.' Whether this should be as

[5] *N.T.S.*, Vol. 13, No. 3, pp. 256–7.

great a problem now in these days of psychosomatic medicine is arguable, for most of the miracles recorded in *Acts* are cases of exorcism or physical healing. No doubt some of the stories that came to Luke, like some of the miracle-stories in his gospel, had lost nothing in the telling, and pious regard for the apostles had added its quota of imaginative embellishments. But we cannot eliminate the miracle-stories from *Acts* any more than we can eliminate them from the gospels, and there is no good reason why we should try. For the restoration of wholeness to mind and body in the case of the diseased and the mentally disturbed was done in the name of Jesus by men who had been endowed with His Spirit to continue His work.

Some of the acts of healing which Luke records were performed by the same men who had earlier been given authority by the Master Himself in Galilee to preach the gospel and to heal the sick. What they and other missionaries were now doing in a wider field was part of the same ministry. They were channels of the healing power of Christ. As St. Peter said to the paralysed, bed-ridden Aeneas: Stand up, Jesus Christ heals you (9:34). It is no diminution of our gratitude to God for modern medical science, and the devoted care of all concerned in the work of healing, to say that there is still evidence of the direct and miraculous power of the Spirit to heal, most spectacularly at Lourdes, but also through un-denominational faith-healers and through the interces-sory activity of divine-healing groups in various branches of the Church today. When Luke describes glossalalia and healing miracles as signs of the Holy

Spirit at work in the life of the early Church he is not a credulous simpleton, far less an inventor of pious marvels, but a sober recorder of a particularly rich outcrop of manifestations of the Spirit, which have never since been completely absent from the Church, but which in the unique period of its beginning appeared with unusual intensity.

Prophecy was the third obvious mark of the presence of the Spirit which occurs frequently in Luke's narrative. Akin to speaking with tongues, it had, in Paul's view, a greater value for the edification of the Church, in that although prophets were also ecstatics they were at least intelligible. Prediction of coming events formed part of the prophet's function, as it did in the Old Testament, but by far his greatest contribution in the early Church, again as in the Old Testament, was inspired preaching, preaching that conveyed the unmistakable sense that this was the Word of God and that the preacher was moved by the Spirit. Ecstasy and trance in themselves no more made a man a prophet, whether in Old Testament times or in the early Church, than having a hand big enough to stretch an octave and two makes a man a great pianist today.

In less startling and unfamiliar ways than have just been described, the Spirit is shown by Luke to have been the main driving-force in the day-to-day life of the earliest Christians. It was the Spirit who gave the apostles, these 'uneducated ordinary men' as Luke calls them (4:13), that extraordinary 'boldness' which enabled them to face the threats of the Sanhedrin with equanimity, who strengthened them to meet persecu-

tion not with resignation but with exultation, who gave
the young community so close a sense of fellowship that
it instituted a common fund for the relief of the poorer
members, who led it to make its criterion of a good
man, like Barnabas, for example, that he was 'full of the
Holy Spirit and of faith' (11 : 24).

On occasion there is mention of the 'comfort' of the
Holy Spirit (9 : 31), and no doubt this was a real element
in early Christian experience as it is today. But the Holy
Spirit administers different kinds of comfort. I remember the present Archbishop of Canterbury, in a public
lecture on the Holy Spirit as the Comforter, drawing
attention to a scene in the Bayeux tapestry where
William the Conqueror is shown marching behind his
troops with a drawn sword in his hand, apparently
prodding them onwards. The legend underneath is:
'King William comforteth his soldiers.' As often as not
in the life of the early Church it was this kind of
comfort that the Spirit provided.

Throughout the whole story of *Acts* we are given the
impression that it was not far-sighted statesmanship
that brought the first Jewish-Christians to the realisa-
tion that the whole world was their parish. Rather we
get a picture of men as prone to religious conservatism
as the main body of the Church has always been, as tied
to their own past history and tradition, as reluctant to
venture out into the unknown future with its problems
and uncertainties, but driven almost against their will
by the unmistakable urge of the Spirit to venture forward into uncharted and intimidating waters with only
their faith to sustain them. Luke shows us that if they

had been left to themselves the members of the first Christian community might well have begun and ended as a little coterie of orthodox Jews, content to meet and celebrate the coming of the Messiah within the confines of the Holy City. But the Spirit moved Stephen to public utterance about the role of Christ in the wider world as it had been revealed to him. In consequence he became the first Christian martyr, but through his protest his supporters were forced, this time certainly against their will, to leave their homes and to take refuge wherever they could. But no matter where they went they were moved to plant the seed of the gospel, and other little Christian communities began to appear up and down the eastern Mediterranean lands.

It was the Spirit, we are told, who prompted Philip the evangelist to accost the God-fearing African official riding south along the Gaza road, and to baptise him after instruction as the first member of the Church from outside the tradition of Israel. It was the Spirit who forced the reluctant Peter to recognise that the Church must embrace Gentiles as well as Jews, beginning with so unlikely a convert in Jewish eyes as an officer of the imperial army. When the more cautious apostles at Jerusalem heard with some dismay of this and of the conversion of large numbers of Samaritans, these ancient enemies of all good Jews, their doubts were silenced by indisputable evidence that the Holy Spirit was pressing them to acknowledge as brothers in Christ people who by every natural inclination they would have preferred to regard as beyond the pale.

So in the rest of his story, which covers the great

expansion of the Church from its Palestinian setting through Asia Minor, Greece and finally to Rome, Luke shows that it was nothing but the prodding of this uncomfortable Comforter, the Spirit, that urged on St. Paul and his associates, despite hazard and opposition, illness, mob-violence and rough justice, to spread the gospel not always where they wanted, but where they were meant to go. It is a moving and exhilarating account, which leaves us in humble wonderment that men of ordinary flesh and blood could endure and survive and still press on with what they believed to be their God-given assignment, a story that is only explicable in the light of the supernatural power with which they were endowed.

This is the point and this is the mood in which we begin to wonder whether Luke's whole story of the first three momentous decades of the Church's history is not too good to be true. This inspiring procession of men and women wholly dedicated to the service of Christ and the furthering of His Kingdom, this impressive evidence of the fellowship of all believers, their compassion and care for one another, their joy in tribulation, their unwavering confidence in the good outcome of their enterprise despite all setbacks, their firm conviction of the divine origin of their faith—can we, as we look at ourselves in the Church today, be persuaded that there ever was such a beginning to our present theological uncertainties, our interdenominational embroilments, our hesitant moral witness, our involvement, in Jesus' words, in 'the cares of this world, the deceitfulness of riches, and the lust of other things' (*Mark*

4:19)? In such a mood we might well conclude either that Luke's picture is a flight of fancy, an ideal that never existed, or that he is describing a state of affairs so far removed from twentieth-century realities that his book has virtually nothing to say to us.

This is no new problem. The contrast between first beginnings and later developments was felt very early in Christian history, but the right conclusions were not necessarily drawn. Eusebius, for example, writing in the fourth century A.D., looks back wistfully and says: In the first epoch of its history, the Church was 'a pure and incorrupt virgin. If there were any who tried to corrupt the sound doctrine of the preaching of salvation, they still hid in a dark hiding place. But when the sacred chorus of the apostles in various ways departed from life, as well as the generation of those who were deemed worthy to hear their inspired wisdom, then also the faction of godless error arose by the deceit of teachers of another doctrine.'

Conzelmann makes the wry comment: 'This is a picture, an idea, not historical reality. In history there was error in the Church from its beginning. There never was such a sacred chorus. There was faith and weakness, there was God's message and men's error—there was: Church in history.'[6] One might suspect indeed that Eusebius had never read the book of *Acts*, for Luke certainly gives no countenance to such an idyllic conception of the first chapter of the Church's story. Luke had himself known some members of the

[6] *The Bible in Modern Scholarship*, J. P. Hyatt (ed.) (London, 1966), pp. 225–6.

'sacred chorus', and he belonged to the generation of those who, according to Eusebius, 'were deemed worthy to hear their inspired wisdom'. He certainly testifies that the gospel of salvation was soundly proclaimed, and that this was well reflected in the quality of the day-to-day life of the Church, but he does not shrink from showing us the seamy side as well.

He does not draw a veil over the wrangling in the Jerusalem congregation concerning the distribution of poor relief, or the plain dishonesty of Ananias and Sapphira. He faithfully records the suspicion with which Paul had to contend within the Church after his conversion, on account of his past black record, the official criticism of Peter for stepping out of line in admitting an officer of the Roman army into the jealously guarded circle of the faithful, and for mixing generally with these impossible Gentiles. Nor does Luke disguise the fact that Mark left Paul's missionary team just as they were getting under way in their first great evangelistic enterprise, and that his defection led later to a violent quarrel between Paul and Mark's kinsman Barnabas. Our author does not pretend that there was not hot, and no doubt bitter, debate at the Council of Jerusalem on the question of whether Gentiles should be allowed to become full members of the Church without submitting to circumcision and accepting other traditional Jewish tenets, nor does he gloss over the likewarm reception which the Apostle to the Gentiles received on his last visit to the Jewish-Christian mother-church at Jerusalem, a church which he had always fallen over backwards to placate, and continued to placate right to the end, for the sake of the unity of Christ's Church.

Luke is thus not describing a Church that never was, a paradise on earth peopled by haloed saints, but a Church where there was as there has always been, in Conzelmann's words: 'faith and weakness', 'God's message and men's error'. It would seem to me that this is the crowning evidence of the general reliability of the story that the book of *Acts* has to tell. If Luke had been, as many recent writers have suggested, a late first-century or early second-century theologian, looking back at the foundation of the Church which he loved, but of whose early beginnings he had no direct knowledge, he would surely have painted a more glamorous picture of the first generation. Instead of that he shows us 'a band of men, whose hearts God had touched' (I *Sam.* 10 : 26), but who were still sinners in need of daily repentance and daily forgiveness.

Similarly, if Luke had been, as has been suggested, a convinced exponent of primitive catholicism, reflecting back into the life of the first Christian decades the more developed ecclesiastical system of the end of the first century, or the beginning of the second, surely he would have left us a tidier canvas. We might have been shown the Twelve Apostles directing the expansion of the Church from Jerusalem, ordaining a proper ministry, formulating a body of doctrine, exercising strict discipline, and handing on their authority to duly-appointed successors. Instead of that Luke gives us both doctrinally and ecclesiastically a thoroughly untidy picture, and the most obvious explanation of that is that this is how it was, and that Luke knew it at first hand to have been so. Perhaps a man who wrote a book which can be called the 'Gospel of the Holy Spirit' understood better than most of us what our Lord meant when He said: 'The wind bloweth where it listeth' (*John* 3:8).

The storm centre of New Testament criticism over the past few decades has been of course the 'Jesus of History' controversy, the question of how much, if anything, we can learn about Him from the gospels, the problem of disentangling what the Church believed about Jesus from what Jesus actually did and said. There is no doubt that many of the insights of Form-criticism are here to stay, and that some at any rate of Bultmann's arguments for demythologising certain elements in the gospels cannot be ignored. What has been most striking, however, and to some of us most welcome, is the recognition in more recent years on the part of some of Bultmann's disciples that his radical criticism had gone too far, and in the so-called 'New Quest of the Historical Jesus', scholars such as Günther Bornkamm are advocating a much more positive evaluation of the historical reliability of the gospel narratives than would have been thought likely a short time ago. This is not simply a case of turning the clock back and reverting to some view of the literal infallibility of scripture from which we have happily escaped. It is, one may believe, a more careful reappraisal of the evidence as a consequence of honest examination of all sides of the question in scholarly debate.

The present focusing of interest on Lucan studies, particularly on the book of *Acts*, cannot be said to be of comparable significance. It is crucial for any preacher or teacher of Christianity to know that he has good reasons for believing that the record of the words and deeds of Jesus in the gospels is generally trustworthy and not simply the product of the Church's faith. The same importance cannot be attached to the reliability of Luke's narrative in *Acts*. Our grounds for Christian belief would not be disastrously undermined if it could be shown conclusively that St. Paul did not address the philosophers of Athens on Mars' Hill in the words which Luke attributes to him, or if for various reasons it appeared more likely that St. Peter restored Dorcas to health rather than to life (9: 36 ff.). On the other hand it is vital for Christian faith to be confident that the substance of Jesus' teaching in the Sermon on the Mount comes from our Lord Himself and that His Resurrection is a fact and not a fairy-tale.

Nevertheless, it is of major concern, and not merely of interest, for the life of the Church and of the ordinary Christian to be able to turn to the book of *Acts* as substantially the true story of our origins, of how the faith we profess was first proclaimed, of how the first Christians viewed the role of the Church in the world, how they lived and worshipped, how they organised their community life, how they preserved their sense of belonging to the same body. I have maintained in these lectures that we have very strong grounds for treating the book of *Acts* with the utmost respect as a basically accurate account of what happened, recorded by a man whose evidence we have good cause to trust. Despite the recent weight of scholarly opinion which would question this judgment, there is a sufficiently large body of reputable scholars who support the traditional view to entitle us to hope that, as in the case of the gospels, a more widespread recognition of the general historical reliability of *Acts* may re-emerge in the not too distant future.

The value of the picture of the life of the earliest stage of Church history that Luke gives us does not lie in the fact that it provides a pattern of organisation and practice which we must try to reproduce in the twentieth century. These first thirty years were in many respects unique, dominated by the recent occurrence of the unique events in the life, death and Resurrection of Jesus, the unique contribution of the men who had been His disciples, and the unique gift of His Spirit at Pentecost. Moreover, the conditions and problems of tiny isolated groups of believers, amid a welter of competing faiths, have obviously more affinity nowadays to the situation of the younger off-shoots of the Church overseas than to the conditions and problems of older branches of the Church with centuries of history and tradition behind them, the consequences of which for good and ill are only too apparent to all of us who belong to them. In a progressively technological society, where the old foundations have been shaken, and new ones have not yet appeared, where the scepticism of scientists and the ineffectualness of philosophers are coupled with the sheer irrelevance of much of the Church's activity, it is little wonder that even thinking Christians begin to talk of the post-Christian era and wonder if the Faith and the Church have any future.

At the risk of appearing to emulate the role of *Athanasius contra mundum,* I want to end these lectures on a more positive note. I feel strongly that against all current trends we must affirm our belief in a transcendent God who has disclosed His nature and purpose as recorded in Holy Scripture and above all in the Person of Jesus Christ. By the same token we must also continue to affirm that Jesus Himself founded the Church and that it is a divine institution against which, however we interpret the words, the gates of hell will not prevail. When we turn to the book of *Acts* we see Christ's purpose beginning to be fulfilled. We see the Church of the earliest days deeply conscious of being the channel of His Spirit as I believe it still is today. But we find in the book of *Acts* no prescribed form or order through which the first Christians believed that the Spirit must be channelled. On the basis of the evidence of *Acts* the Spirit is as likely nowadays to come to men and women through the tambourines and joyful choruses of the Salvation Army in a dreary little mission hall as through the solemn magnificence of High Mass in a Roman basilica.

But let us be quite clear about our frontiers in view of present theological trends. The book of *Acts* does not encourage us to see in other religious, Judaism or Hellenistic faiths—and in our own day this would have to be widened to include the great world religions of Buddhism, Islam, Hinduism as well as scientific humanism—anything more than a *praeparatio evangelica.* Let us seek to establish what we have in common with all of them and co-operate as far as we may. But the Incarna-

tion was an event in history, as was Christ's foundation
of His Church. Unless we are prepared to dismiss the
evidence of Scripture, the Church is God's means of
bringing the world to the knowledge of the truth about
Himself, about man's destiny and about the purpose of
Creation. In this sense it is true that outside the Church
there is no salvation.

But in the light of Luke's record in *Acts* there is nothing sacrosanct about the present form of the Church
in any of its branches. It was launched into the world as
the community of the Holy Spirit and it opened its
doors to all and sundry on the simple basis of their
acceptance of Jesus Christ as Saviour and Lord. Subsequently organisation and discipline became necessary
but none of this was of the essence of its origins, for the
unity of the earliest Christians was based on quite a
modest four-fold formula: faith in Christ in accordance
with the apostolic teaching, the fellowship of all believers issuing in social action, regular sacramental
observance and common prayer (2:42). It was on such
an unpretentious basis of unity that the Church began.
Have we any right to make the conditions of membership of a reunited Church any more difficult now?

But of course the unity of the Church for which, as
Luke shows us, St. Paul fought so valiantly was then,
and is still, only a means to an end, which is a fact that
one feels is sometimes lost sight of in ecumenical discus-
sions. The sole purpose of the Church in the mind of
the first Christians was undoubtedly to win the world
for Christ. The ways in which the Church can best fulfil
this mission have varied widely, under the leading of

the Spirit, over the past two thousand years, and will doubtless vary even more widely until God's purpose is finally accomplished. But if we are to be guided by the book of *Acts*, whatever techniques of mission the Church may use, in the last resort it exists in the world to summon men and women to commit their lives to God through Christ, and to enable them as part of one great family to become the sons and daughters of God that they were meant to be.